SCIENCE AND THE SACRED

SCIENCE AND THE SACRED
ETERNAL WISDOM IN A CHANGING WORLD

A NEW, REVISED, AND ABRIDGED EDITION

RAVI RAVINDRA

Quest Books
Theosophical Publishing House
Wheaton, Illinois ◆ Chennai (Madras), India

The Theosophical Society acknowledges with gratitude the generous support of the Kern Foundation for the publication of this book.

First Quest Edition 2002
Originally published 2000
Theosophical Publishing House, Adyar, Chennai, India
Theosophical Publishing House, Wheaton, Illinois

The Theosophical Publishing House
P. O. Box 270
Wheaton, Illinois 60189-0270

Library of Congress Cataloging-in-Publication Data

Ravindra, Ravi.
Science and the sacred: eternal wisdom in a changing world / Ravi Ravindra.—New, rev. and abridged ed.
p.   cm.
Includes bibliographical references.
ISBN 0-8356-0820-4
1. Religion and science.   I. Title.

BL241 .R325 2002
291.1'75—dc21

2002068388

5   4   3   2   1   *   02   03   04   05   06   07   08

Printed in the United States of America

Koham kathamidam cheti samsāramalamātatam
pravichāryam prayatnena prājñena sahasādhunā

    Who am I?
Whence is this widespread cosmic flux?
These, the wise should inquire into diligently,
Soon—nay, now.

                              (Mahopanishad 4.21)

CONTENTS

PREFACE

"It is no exaggeration to say," remarked A. N. Whitehead (180), "that the future course of history depends on the decision of this generation as to the relations between religion and science." Initially, some are likely to think that science simply means knowledge, as it does etymologically, and that any reasonable and systematic study of phenomena is science. It is easy to forget that there are certain basic presuppositions of scientific inquiry in the modern (post-sixteenth-century) world, essentially derived from a particular stage in European philosophical and religious history, which set modern science apart not only from the sciences of China and India but also from the ancient European sciences. These presuppositions involve the very essence of what makes any culture distinctive from another, namely issues dealing with such questions as the place and meaning of human beings in the cosmos, the nature and aim of knowledge, the relevance and importance of external experiments and internal experiences in providing data and evidence, and the value and significance of faith in the development of science.

It is not very easy to come to an agreement on what a phenomenon is, and certainly not on what is reasonable, and therefore on what science is. For example, in a recent conference, there was a question repeatedly raised by some Eastern intellectuals about whether a systematic internal investigation of various subtle energies in the human body is a scientific study. Is Yoga a science? The hesitation of the Western intellectuals in agreeing on an affirmative answer to that question is understandable, because science is not just any reasonable and systematic study of phenomenon, as one may be tempted to think. It is a particular kind of study that is based on identifiable philosophical assumptions and worldviews, that requires external evidence independent of the level of

9

spiritual development of the researcher, and that is subject to repeatability, prediction, and control.

These considerations and difficulties, involving the nature of reason and the specific rationality underlying scientific procedures, are germane to the extremely important question of the relationship of science and spirit. Of course, it is even more difficult to clearly define what spirit is. However, one remark may be made here: Traditional knowledge asserts that spirit is higher than and prior to body-mind, sometimes for simplicity called only "body." Even though various spiritual traditions may express the concept differently, they can all understand and endorse the essence of the proposition "In the beginning was the Spirit."

Two very closely related comments need to be made about the difference between the "spiritual" and the "scientific" perspectives, keeping in mind the difficulties associated with such generalizations. First, for the most part, spiritual traditions assert that "it is the spirit that has the body." On the other hand, from the scientific point of view, if spirit can be spoken of at all, it can only be that "it is the body that has the spirit." Vast philosophic and cultural differences are implied in these expressions. Second, by and large, the scientific motivation for an inquiry into the relationship between science and spirit seems to be "How can the spiritual energy be utilized in doing better science that will lead to a more useful technology?" The spiritual point of view, on the other hand, seems to be "How can science, or anything else, be of service to the spirit?"

We can happily agree that spirituality is universal, nonsectarian, and not restricted to the East or the West. Spirituality is not limited by geographical, historical, or sectarian divisions. It is also clear that spirituality does not have much to do with a belief system or doctrine, theological arguments and proofs, or enthusiastic evangelism. It is primarily a quality of being, reflected in bodily stillness, in emotional generosity, and in compassion, no less than in mental clarity and serenity—a quality that represents a further evolution of the human being. Spirituality has to do with a new birth, a transformation of consciousness, or a raising of the level of awareness—all this leading to a different person who is born into and manifests a new mode of being, almost a different species.

In every aspect of a human being, there is a wide range of variation of quality. Intellectual capacity ranges from a moron to a genius. Physical strength and flexibility ranges from a sickly person to an athlete. In the realm of spirituality, the variations are subtler and more profound, touching the very core of a person and that person's destiny and significance. Spiritual profundity is not a matter of a particular accomplishment; it is concerned with the quality of the whole of the person and with nearness to the spirit.

In the light of the above, it is not surprising that the sages, saints, and mystics should have a great deal of difficulty in communicating with other human beings about their spiritual experiences. These are no more than the expected difficulties in what amounts to practically an interspecies communication. However, virtually every spiritual tradition maintains that all members of the species *Homo sapiens* have the potentiality of being in touch with faculties that are specifically spiritual (as distinct from mental, emotional, or physical) and that these faculties, even when undeveloped, do in some measure correspond to what the sages have said about them. Therefore, even when we do not quite understand what the sages are saying, we find it difficult to wholly ignore them; something subtle whispers in our ears, sometimes quite in spite of ourselves.

In order to understand the sages and scriptures spiritually, we need to undergo a change of being or a rebirth or a cleansing of our perceptions. An intellectual and physical (that is, scientific) understanding neither requires any transformation of our being nor can lead to such a transformation. Neither scientific knowledge about people who have spiritual knowledge nor theoretical knowledge about the spirit makes one a sage.

If the notion of the spiritual and the corresponding possibilities of enlightenment, freedom, or salvation are taken seriously, then what is spiritual is almost by definition, as well as by universal consensus, higher than what is intellectual. The intellect is contained in being, as a part in the whole, and not the other way around.

There are many perspectives from which one may explore the issues between science and spirituality. The present author wishes to remain true to the universal insight and assertion of the mystics and other spiritual masters that spirit is above the mind. Of course, many other words have been used other than "Spirit" to indicate Higher Reality, such as God, Brahman, the One, Tao, the Buddha Mind, and the like. Furthermore, it has been universally said that in order to come to know this Higher

Reality in truth, a transformation of the whole being of the seeker is needed to yoke and quiet the mind so that, without any distortions, it may reflect what is brought about by fear and fantasy.

Paraphrasing Saint Paul (1 Corinthians 2.11–4), it can be said that the things of the mind can be understood by the mind, but those of the spirit can be understood only by the spirit. It is this spiritual part in a person that needs to be cultivated for the sake of spiritual knowledge. In some traditions, this spiritual part, which like a magnetic compass always tries to orient itself to the north pole of the spirit, is called "soul." This part alone, when properly cultivated, can comprehend and correspond to the suprapersonal and universal spirit. Any other kind of knowledge can be about the spirit but cannot be called knowing the spirit.

If a label is needed for the approach taken in this book, it is not "philosophical" or "historical" or "scientific"; it is above all "spiritual"—with all the attendant vagueness and need for clarification—in which spirit is given priority. In this perspective, the question cannot be "How can I appropriate the spirit?" The only real and worthy question is "How can I—and along with me, my science—be appropriated by the spirit?" Such an attitude of spiritual humility is not wholly alien to all scientists; for some of the greatest among them, science itself has been a spiritual path, a way—as Einstein said—of finding the secrets of the Old One.

RAVI RAVINDRA

Acknowledgments

Some of the chapters in this volume originally appeared, in different forms, in the following sources:

"Ancient Wisdom in a Changing World," *American Theosophist* 71 (1983): 331–7.

"Modern Science and Spiritual Traditions," *Journal of Science and Technology* 9 (1996): 92–9.

"Perception in Yoga and Physics," *Re-Vision, Journal of Knowledge and Consciousness* 3 (spring 1980): 36–42.

"Western Science and Technology and the Indian Intellectual Tradition," *Manthan* September 1978, 8–16.

"Yoga and Knowledge," *Science and Spirit*, by Ravi Ravindra (New York: Paragon House, 1991), 267–77.

"Experience and Experiment: A Critique of Modern Scientific Knowing," *Dalhousie Review* 55 (1975–6): 655–74.

"In the Beginning Is the Dance of Love," *Origin and Evolution of the Universe: Evidence for Design?* ed. J. M. Robson (Montreal: McGill University Press, 1987), 259–79.

"To the Dancer Belongs the Universe: Freedom and Bondage of Natural Law," *Science and Spirit*, by Ravi Ravindra (New York: Paragon House, 1991), 329–50.

"Science as a Spiritual Path," *Journal of Religious Studies* 7 (1979): 78–85.

"A Science of Inner Transformation," *Holistic Science and Human Values*, Theosophy Science Centre, Transactions 2, 1997, pp. 119–26.

"Science and the Mystery of Silence," *American Theosophist* 70 (1982): 350–5.

The author gratefully acknowledges a Senior Fellowship from the Shastri Indo-Canadian Institute and a Leave Fellowship from the Social Sciences and Humanities Research Council of Canada for writing "Western Science and Technology and the Indian Intellectual Tradition." He is also thankful for the hospitality extended by the Department of Religion, Punjabi University, Patiala, and the Indian Institute of Advanced Study, Shimla. Prof. T. R. V. Murty was very generous with his time in Varanasi and very patient with questions about the philosophies of India.

Some of the ideas in "Experience and Experiment—A Critique of Modern Scientific Knowing" arose in response to various remarks made by Professors Eugene P. Wigner, John A. Wheeler, Thomas S. Kuhn, and Walter Kaufman in seminars or private discussions when the author was a Visiting Fellow at Princeton University in the Program for History and Philosophy of Science, on a Canada Council Post-Doctoral Fellowship in Philosophy in 1968–69. Much of it was written during 1973–74 at Columbia University, where I was a Visiting Scholar in Religion on a Fellowship for Cross-Disciplinary Studies awarded by the Society for Religion in Higher Education. An earlier version of the essay was presented, in a considerably different form, at a meeting in Toronto of the Canadian Society for the Study of Religion in May, 1974. I have had the benefit of discussions with Professor W. Nicholls of the University of British Columbia, Mr. Arvind Sharma of Harvard University, and Professors Wilfred Cantwell Smith, A. Hilary Armstrong, and Robert H. March of Dalhousie University. My friend Robert L. McWhinney was very helpful in his editorial advice. A research grant from Dalhousie University is gratefully acknowledged.

The author is very grateful to John Algeo for undertaking the careful editing and pruning of the original publication in order to produce this abridged and more accessible version.

CHAPTER ONE

ANCIENT WISDOM
IN A CHANGING WORLD

In a Sufi story, Jesus, son of Mary, met an old man on a mountain, who lived in the open air without shelter against heat and cold. "Why dost thou not build a house?" Jesus asked him.

"O Spirit of God," replied the old man, "prophets before thee predicted that I would live for only seven hundred years; therefore it is not worth my trouble to settle down."

This tale, told by Safuri, a writer of the fifteenth century, is a good reminder that time and change are extremely relative matters. For the old man on the mountain, seven hundred years were short, whereas for us moderns seven years would be long. The old man perhaps had the perspective of an everlasting eternity, which dwarfs all things of time, however enduring or valuable. We, on the other hand, measure by the number of changes that crowd a unit of time. We judge even eternity by the standards of interesting changes in time. We dare to wish for eternal life when even a Sunday afternoon drags too slowly for us!

Perhaps, however, the old man in the story misunderstood the nature of *eternity* as contrasted with *time*. Perhaps he thought of eternal life as a life of endless duration, as time that lasts forever, rather than as a state of being in time that is accompanied by the qualities of perception and love. Eternity is worth spending a little time to consider. *Eternity*—one can hardly utter the word without wonder, reflection, and inward silence. Whenever our contemplation deepens and our thought matures, what concerns serious people is eternity. Yet the pull of time, even with respect to eternity, is very strong.

The closing pages of Herman Hesse's novel *Steppenwolf* include the following dialog:

"Time and the world, money and power belong to the small people and the shallow people. To the rest, to the real men belongs nothing. Nothing but death."

"Nothing else?"

"Yes, eternity."

"You mean a name, and fame with posterity?"

"No, Steppenwolf, not fame. Has that any value? And do you think that all true and real men have been famous and known to posterity?"

"No, of course not."

"Then it isn't fame. Fame exists in that sense only for the schoolmasters. No, it isn't fame. It is what I call eternity. The pious call it the kingdom of God. I say to myself: all we who ask too much and have a dimension too many could not continue to live at all if there were not another air to breathe outside the air of this world, if there were not eternity at the back of time; and this is the kingdom of truth."

In this passage, we have a hint of two distinct concepts of *eternity*. One is a continuation in time; this eternity means forever, endless, without break in time, ceaseless, everlasting. It is essentially a linear notion in which time is a quantitative extension to infinity. This is the common understanding of the word, wittily expressed in a popular cookbook as "eternity: two people and a ham!"

In the second understanding, unlike in the first, there is a qualitative difference between *time* and *eternity*. *Eternal* is thus *timeless*, not in the sense that it occurs in zero time, instantaneously, but rather in the sense that it pertains to a dimension of being (including consciousness and perception) other than that of time. This eternity is an attribute of being, but it is not a concept, simply because the mind functions only in time. One cannot *think* about eternity or timelessness—as Kant pointed out long ago, as have many others both before and after him. Jiddu Krishnamurti (*Commentaries on Living* 233) has rightly said, "Thought cannot know the timeless; it is not a further acquisition, a further achievement; there is no going towards it. It is a state of being in which thought, time, is not."

Everlasting and *timeless* are two understandings of what is *eternal;* and they lie in different spheres of experience. Everlasting is not timeless. Anything that is everlasting is still within the finite-infinite dichotomy, whereas timelessness transcends this contradiction, for the category of time does not apply to it (Ravindra, "Is the Eternal Everlasting?").

ANCIENT WISDOM

Why are we at all interested in ancient wisdom? Is our interest largely antiquarian? Or chauvinistic? Is something true simply or largely because it is ancient? Without question, great truths were enunciated in ancient times and at many places. But of course great truths can also be enunciated now or in the future.

To imagine, based on some theory of time cycles or *yugas* or revelation, that there cannot be a fresh revelation or a new manifestation of divinity or further profound enunciations of truth is to set quite uncalled for limits on the creative outpourings of the Holy Spirit. The fact that most of the followers of great religions and great prophets have behaved as if there were such limits on the Holy Spirit is an expression of ordinary human mentality, which wishes to possess a given form of Truth—in spite of the presence of great wisdom at all times.

When we speak of the "ancient wisdom," the emphasis does not need to be on the word "ancient." Of course, truths that have stood the test of time naturally recommend themselves. Again and again, in varying forms and with shifts of emphasis, some truths are rediscovered and restated. For example, the truth that the major operating principles in the world, at least on the human level, are fear and craving has been seen and stated many times by great teachers. Each time the emphasis is a little different: Sometimes the root of our inner and outer suffering is said to be our fears and cravings; sometimes the very entity we call "myself" is said to be made up of our fears and cravings; sometimes our lower self or self-will or ego is identified with these, as distinct from the real "I" or Atman or Self. But in any case, the fact that we are driven by fear and craving remains. It is an enduring truth about ourselves; it is an eternal truth, in one of the senses of that word discussed above.

However much the world changes, the truth about fear and craving remains, simply because it refers to the cosmological level of our world and provides its psychological nexus. However many accelerated and

17

wonderful changes have come about, and will no doubt come about in the scientific, technological, and sociological realms of the future, this truth will remain as a truth about ourselves. And whenever we, the greatly learned and innovative among us or the not-so learned and not-so "with-it," are called or even forced to look at ourselves seriously, we see this truth. It does not matter whether our scientific paradigms are Newtonian, Einsteinian, holographic or anything else—this truth does not change; it defines our world and the underlying principle of its working.

What also does not change is our wish to be free of our fears and cravings—dimly felt often, strongly felt occasionally, and undertaken as a practical project rarely. We don't know what else can be, other than these; we cling to the security of this shore lest there be no other shore. On this very shore, we walk up and down, picking up this pebble or that for examination, changing this paradigm or that.

Clearly, at its own level, there is nothing wrong with this shore; it too is needed. There is nothing wrong with the enjoyment that one derives from the changing scientific and technological scene; this very world is after all the world of action. The question however arises: With what level of being—that is, with what degree of freedom from fear and craving—does one engage with the world and its varied and wonderful activities? All activities—scientific, artistic, social, and others—reflect our level of being, our fears and means for protection, our cravings and means for gratification. But, like Steppenwolf, some of us "have a dimension too many," a dimension not opposed to but different from that of time and action, the dimension of eternity and being.

> Men's curiosity searches past and future
> And clings to that dimension. But to apprehend
> The point of intersection of the timeless
> With time, is an occupation for the saint—
> No occupation either, but something given
> And taken, in a lifetime's death in love,
> Ardour and selflessness and self-surrender.
> For most of us, there is only the unattended
> Moment, the moment in and out of time,
> The distraction fit, lost in a shaft of sunlight,
> The wild thyme unseen, or the winter lightning

Or the waterfall, or music heard so deeply
That it is not heard at all, but you are the music
While the music lasts. These are only hints and guesses,
Hints followed by guesses; and the rest
Is prayer, observance, discipline, thought and action.

(T. S. Eliot, "The Dry Salvages")

The major concern of wisdom, which itself is timeless but which has been since ancient times, is the point of intersection of the timeless with time. It is not opposed to time or the things of time. As the Maitri Upanishad (6.15) succinctly says, "There are verily two forms of Brahman (the Vastness and the Real), Kala (time) and Akala (timelessness)." Wisdom is concerned with freedom from the hold of time, from the conditionings of the past and the imaginings of the future. In that state of being, one can act freely and freshly in time, and see that Nirvana is *kala-vimukta:* Nirvana is freedom from time. Thus, wisdom, ancient or modern or future, acts in time to assist the transformation of anyone who wishes and is able and willing to pay the price, so that one can act in time while being anchored in eternity. The blue god of the mysterious vastness, sometimes called Krishna, makes love to the pale Radha of time; and fecundates her with multiplicity and decorates her with wondrous ornaments!

We can easily see the reason why so many of the spiritual traditions, which naturally are concerned with wisdom, lay so much emphasis on paying attention to the present moment, on being here and now. "Now" is the point of intersection of time and eternity. "If we take eternity to mean not infinite temporal duration but timelessness, then eternal life belongs to those who live in the present" (Wittgenstein, proposition 6.4311). In practice, one sees the difficulty of staying in the present, the eternal now, in the face of the strong momentum of time. The greatest weapon Māra (the deadly tempter) has, in his war against anyone wishing to wake up from the hypnotic sleep in which we all live with fearing and craving, is time and temporal power and the enchanting imaginings transporting us away from the now and the real. A dialogue between a monk and a Zen master illustrates this concept:

Monk: In order to work in the Tao is there a special way?

Master: Yes, there is one.

Monk: Which is it?

Master: When one is hungry, one eats: When one is tired, one sleeps.

Monk: That is what everybody does; is their way the same as yours?

Master: It is not the same.

Monk: Why not?

Master: When they eat they do not only eat, they weave all sorts of imaginings. When they sleep they give rein to a thousand idle thoughts. That is why their way is not my way.

CHANGING WORLD

We live at a moment of great opportunity; it is difficult to remain parochial. A special sort of imperviousness and insecurity are needed these days, for us who live in the global village, to ignore the existence of other great cultures. There are various modes of approaching reality—other religions, other kinds of music, other visual sensibilities, other modes of thought—all quite different from those to which we are accustomed. Some are different at their very roots, others only partly so. In some, the same questions are asked but with unexpected emphases; in others, wholly different questions are raised. Some people brought up in other cultures wonder why we are preoccupied with the questions we ask and the practices we follow.

On a smaller scale, of course, this variety has always existed. There have been other peoples, many much more intelligent and serious than ourselves, whose concerns and ideals have been different from ours. Yet our neighborhood is now, for many of us, considerably enlarged, bringing us into contact with diverse ways of being in the world and other points of view shaped by different environments, histories, languages, and traditions. For that reason, a fundamental and radical self-questioning is more necessary and perhaps a little easier.

If we do not dismiss those who are different from ourselves simply as stupid, insensitive, misguided, or damned, our cultural and religious self-exile can be justified only by our ignorance, or by a conviction that we are already in possession of the ultimate truth or the way to it, or by a lack of energy and a real wish to examine and understand our own culture and thereby ourselves. We can hardly know ourselves in isolation from others; we can hardly know our own culture, in its presuppositions and preoccupations, without encountering other cultures. As between individuals, so between cultures: Real knowledge of the other and thereby of oneself, arises and flourishes largely in a state of love. Otherwise, it is difficult to escape the covert control of one by the other, whether the control and manipulation are religious, economic, or conceptual.

What is true of other human beings and other cultures is true also of other times. In the midst of the present-day cultural pluralism, when all levels of texts, practices, and techniques are available from various cultures and times, it is easy to lose objectivity, with respect to oneself or others. It is clearly silly to assume that we have the truth and others don't, an underlying assumption of all missionary attitudes; but it is also naive to believe that other cultures, groups, or times have the truth and we don't. Similarly, whereas it is patently absurd to imagine that wisdom began with Copernicus (a well-known scientist once asked me with some surprise, "You mean, it didn't?")—as if the ancients were just savages—it is certainly merely romantic to imagine that all the ancients were full of wisdom and harmony, but now we have lost it all.

One can focus on a macroscopic view of another culture or time and compare it with a microscopic view of one's own. Similarly, one can maintain an ideal picture of another religion and contrast it with the actual reality of one's own. This perspective indicates a lack of appreciation of the seriousness of our common human difficulties, as well as of the scale of the forces at work. This view can lull us into thinking that the transforming of our times, our cultures, or ourselves can be done quickly, by fixing this or that fault, of which we have become aware by comparison with others.

Human beings everywhere, at all times and in all civilizations, seem to be constantly subject to vast forces, crisscrossing in their upward and downward tendencies. In general, the mass of any civilization drags its center of gravity downwards, only occasionally to be lifted up by the spiritually wise who understand their mission, involving effort and suffering for the sake of maintaining the right cosmic order.

As in our own time and culture, so in others: They too, at their best, respond to the call from above; and, exactly like us, they too often forget the flame of truth, repeat rituals and slogans mechanically, give way to baser passions, and live in exile from grace. There are some among them, as there are some among us, who claim that they are in exclusive possession of truth or salvation. But also, there are some among them so manifestly wise, compassionate, and farseeing that they compel our attention and respect.

In addition to the manifest pluralism of our times, one outstanding feature of the contemporary world is juxtaposition without coherence. All things, all teachings, and all information are available, but we don't know their right significance or place. In the midst of the total availability of everything, there is total disorder—externally and internally. The external disorder is largely a reflection of our internal disorder and chaos. A manifestation of our internal incoherence is that we value both others, of different times or cultures, and ourselves alternately too much or too little.

Cultural styles come and go; we accumulate more or less knowledge about this or that; we live a little longer or a little shorter. All this does not matter very much. The depth is in altogether a different dimension. To be sure, there are cultural styles, institutional forms, or varieties of education that can be more conducive to certain depths, whereas others are less conducive. But the quality of this depth, or the lack of comprehension about it, or the general societal conspiracy of evading it, are not essentially different today than they were in the days of the Buddha or the Christ, nor are they any different in America than in China. They are intimately connected with the well-nigh universal human condition: our persistent wish to live in a dream about ourselves and about others.

All social reforms seem to be essentially attempts to rearrange the contents of our dreams by altering the social institutions that maintain a particular set of these dreams for larger or smaller cultural units. Different cultural units have different dreams, some more pleasant than others, but still they are dreams. What is needed is a questioning of these dreams, a questioning of the very state of dreaming, a questioning of ourselves in our entirety—in relation to the cosmos, to other people, and above all to ourselves.

Such questioning is too radical for us to bear for any length of time—*radical* in the literal meaning of the word, namely what concerns the very roots: the roots of my existence, the roots of my being, and the roots of my possibilities. It is because we wish to escape the radical depths that we engage in arranging and rearranging the surfaces. Lest it should become clear to us how hollow we are, we undertake to reform others according to some ideology, or to convert them to some belief system or a new paradigm. It is much easier to begin to teach others than to realize in one's core that at a very fundamental level one does not know and cannot know, as long as one is what one is.

The primary question is one of being rather than of knowing, of transformation rather than information, of freedom from oneself—from that part of oneself that is a participant in the social dream and therefore lives basically by the operating principles of society, namely reward and punishment, craving and fear.

The world and the times will sometimes be better and sometimes be worse, but always changing. Coming back to the little tale in the beginning of this chapter, whether the time is short or long does not matter. What matters is how one is now. From what depth within oneself does one engage with the surfaces? Wisdom consists, in part, in not building a psychological house while one builds a physical one. Right internal order and real freedom have to be continually regained, from now to now, and do not persist in time as a continued momentum from the past to the future.

A long time ago, and now, Krishna and Radha live by a riverbank as householders. One day they get a message that the sage Durvasa, well-known for his austerities and short temper, is on the other bank with a thousand of his followers, demanding to be fed. As proper householders, Krishna and Radha undertake to do their part in the maintenance of order *(dharma)* by preparing food for the mendicants. When Radha is ready to carry the food across to the other shore, she sees the river in full spate and wonders how she can get across. Krishna says, "Go to the river and say, 'If Krishna is eternally celibate, O River, subside.' " Radha well knows the power of uttering the true word; but is this the true word? Of all people, she ought to know! She smiles to herself, goes to the river, and asks it to subside if Krishna is eternally celibate. The river subsides. She goes across and takes the food to the sage Durvasa, who is well pleased and eats heartily along with his disciples. When it is time for Radha to return, she again sees the river in full spate, and asks the sage for help. The sage says, "Go to the river and say, 'If Durvasa is eternally fasting, O River, subside.'" Radha had just seen the sage eat. She smiles to herself, goes to the river and asks it to subside if Durvasa is eternally fasting. The river subsides and Radha returns home to Krishna.

Modern Science and Spiritual Traditions: A Perspective from India

If modern Western science were the only way to truth, why should we bother about what can be learned from India or China or the Islamic cultures?

Modern science is not the only avenue to truth. Great spiritual traditions all over the world have other perspectives on reality that are based on direct and intuitive perceptions in purified states of consciousness, which are either ignored or denied by science. Among the perceptions achieved in those spiritual traditions is an acknowledgment of levels of being higher than the mind, which can be experienced but cannot be known by any mode of knowledge that separates object and subject. The state of consciousness in which such unitive insight is possible requires a radical transformation of being brought about by spiritual disciplines such as Yoga. Yoga also leads to a theory and practice of natural science on principles that are fundamentally different from those of modern Western science.

When we speak about a great and a vast culture such as China's or India's, we should expect to find in it everything that human beings have thought, felt, and tried anywhere else in the world. So, if we talk about certain specific aspects of a culture, we are not saying that other things do not exist in it as well. However, the great minds of every culture keep returning to particular central insights or essential truths, which are the defining core of that culture.

It is also useful to remember that the great core insights of a culture are only part of the many forces operating on human beings in that culture. Other forces—of history, politics, and economics, of human greed, fear, and competitiveness—still continue to operate in the presence of these great insights.

No culture has a monopoly of wisdom—or of stupidity. When considering the specific greatness of a particular culture, we must not imagine that any one culture alone ought to be emulated and that the others can be abandoned. There is a very apt remark of the Buddha to this effect: "It is not proper for a wise person who holds to the truth to come to the conclusion, 'This alone is Truth, and nothing else.'"

There is nothing ultimately irreconcilable about the East and the West, for human beings brought up in one culture can, at a deep level, understand another culture. At a deep level, human beings can be free of the presuppositions and tendencies of their own culture. However, such freedom does require discovering and operating from very deep layers of consciousness. And that discovery in turn requires immense freedom, compassion, and wisdom, which are to be expected from only a few individuals.

There are several insights that are shared by all the great spiritual traditions of the world. Although here the Indian tradition is singled out for a detailed discussion, it is worthwhile to mention a few points that are shared by all spiritual traditions but are either ignored or contradicted by modern science (Ravindra, *Science and Spirit*, esp. chs. 1, 4, and 5; Nasr, *Encounter of Man and Nature*).

All spiritual traditions assert that there are many levels of being or consciousness within a person, as well as in the cosmos, and that the highest can be experienced only in the deepest part of the soul. Also all the traditions say that there is something—variously called Spirit or God or Allah or Brahman—that is above the mind. It cannot be comprehended by the ordinary mind but can be experienced by human beings whose consciousness has been radically transformed. This transformation constitutes a new birth, a spiritual birth, or a virgin birth, as contrasted with the biological birth resulting from the carnal intercourse of human beings.

Furthermore, according to the spiritual traditions, the purpose of human birth and of all human endeavors, including the sciences and the arts, is to assist individuals to experience Divine Being and to manifest that Being in their lives, to the best of their ability, with love and compassion. In this traditional perspective, science needs to serve the spirit; otherwise, it ends up serving, almost by default, the natural human tendency towards self-centeredness, resulting in violence against and exploitation of other humans, cultures, and creatures, as well as the Earth itself.

THE VISION OF INDIA

The one central insight into Truth to which all Indian wisdom points is the *oneness of all that exists*. This insight is not alien to other cultures; but in India all the great sages again and again return to it. In fact, the realization of this truth is what defines the greatness of a person in India. Although the truth is easily stated as "All is one," the sages have also said that the realization of this truth in the core of one's being can take many lifetimes. And the realization of this truth is held to be the purpose of human existence. All art, philosophy, and science, if they are true, reflect this vision and further its realization.

The truth of fundamental unity has been stated in myriad ways during the long history of India. In the Rig Veda, the earliest text in any Indo-European language, we find this truth in a cosmological-mythological form as the various gods and natural forces transform themselves into each other. In the Upanishads, the supreme identity of Atman and Brahman discovered in meditation indicates the oneness of the deepest level in a person (Atman) with the subtlest and therefore the highest level of the cosmos (Brahman).

The Buddha enunciated this ancient truth freshly when he said that the whole world, including all the gods and all the demons, can be discovered in one's very own body. Mara, the personification of death and every obstructing force, turned out to be a projection of the Buddha's own mind, not something separate and other than him. From Krishna in the Bhagavad Gita, one hears that those who truly know realize that all there is, is Krishna. One and the same Divine energy manifests itself in the various forms engaged in the wonderful dance of *prakriti* or nature, both manifest and unmanifest.

The third-century Buddhist philosopher Nagarjuna expresses the same realization as a negation in the subtle doctrine of *Shunyata* or Emptiness, which asserts that anything in isolation is devoid, not only of significance, but of any reality whatsoever. This applies to everything, including the classical opposites of *nirvana* and *samsara*—thus Nagarjuna's exuberant conclusion that *nirvana* is *samsara* and *samsara* is *nirvana*. The Hindu Vedanta philosopher Shankara expresses the same truth as a positive assertion that only Brahman is real and anything apart from It is nonreal and therefore nonexistent. In our own time, Maharishi Raman has proclaimed, "There are no others," and Jiddu Krishnamurti has spoken about the oneness of the observer and the observed (Ravindra, *Krishnamurti*, esp. the end of ch. 2).

During a period of at least four thousand years—as reckoned by Western scientific chronology—the sages in India have repeatedly asserted the underlying unity of all that exists, including everything we call animate or inanimate, and have said that the cultivation of wisdom consists in the realization of this truth. Furthermore, we can be one with All That Is, precisely because in isolation we are nothing. As the ancient text of the Shatapatha Brahmana (3.8.1.2–3) says, only those may enter the Sun door who can truly answer the question "Who are you?" with "No one." The expressions of this fundamental insight vary in time, but the insight itself is said by the sages to be a part of Eternal Order *(Santana Dharma)*. It not only coexists with the cosmos, but provides its stable foundation.

UNITIVE KNOWLEDGE AND INSIGHT

The root cause of our suffering is our alienation from the All. This alienation is rooted in self-centeredness, which in turn is founded on the illusion of being a separate self with its own projects and purposes apart from those of the cosmos. Individualism, which presupposes an isolated self, inevitably leads to selfishness, exploitation, and violence. Any knowledge or practice that leads to the removal of the illusion of separateness is heading in the right direction. The illusion is sustained by ignorance; therefore what is needed for freedom from this illusion is unitive knowledge and insight *(vidyā or jñāna or prajñā)*.

The primary emphasis in the Indic traditions is on knowledge, unlike in the faith-centered biblical traditions (Ravindra, *Whispers,* esp. ch. 6). However, this knowledge or *jñāna* is quite different from scientific knowledge in its nature and consequences. For example, in *jñāna*, fact and value cannot be separated because the factual reality of anything is essentially a measure of its relationship with the whole, which gives it its value. Also, in science, the quality of the work does not depend on the human qualities of the scientist. There is no requirement that a great scientist like Newton be possessed of large-heartedness, love, or self-sacrifice. On the other hand, if the Buddha is wise or has *jñāna*, to say that he is not compassionate would be a contradiction. We recognize that the Buddha is wise because he is compassionate and because all his behavior, thought, and speech show that he realizes the truth of the essential unity of all.

The sense we have of being separate from each other is, however, also a part of the All and needs not only to be accepted, but also to be understood. It is not something to be eliminated. As we understand more subtly and comprehensively the relationship of the many to the One, we do not cling to the partial vision of separateness, seeing it as the sole reality or even as an important aspect of Reality. The emphasis on separate entities is functional at the ordinary level of existence, but that appearance is not the significant part of the Real. A philosophic mind is naturally more interested in the causes and sources than in the effects, more in the way things are than in the way they appear.

In fact, separateness would seem to be obvious and commonsensical. I am here, you are there. We look different from each other, and our genetic and cultural histories are different, as are our memories and fears. However, one of the useful lessons to be learned from the history of science is that commonsense is not a reliable guide to truth. Most of what physicists came to in the late twentieth century was anything but commonsense. Separateness is there, but it is enfolded in relationships.

An analogy from physics may be helpful. Field theories do not deny the existence of atoms, but they focus their attention on the intervening space and on the energies and fields that inevitably affect the separate atoms. The analogy is not exact because, in physics, the alternative particle and field theoretic descriptions are said to be equivalent whereas, in the cosmologies influenced by the spiritual insight of an underlying unity, the contrasting views of the one and the many are seen as higher and lower perspectives. The emphasis on levels—of consciousness, being, insight, and clarity of perception—is integral to this theory of knowledge. What and how one sees depends on the level of being of the seer.

The unitary insight of the sages is not a matter of universalizing or generalizing from particulars by reasoning, inference, or induction. It is primarily a matter of perception—an actual vision. It is an insight, not a conjecture or an abstraction subject to refutation or confirmation. This perception is possible only when our doors of perception are cleansed of all fear and fantasy. The world a sage sees is not the world an ordinary person sees. It requires the sacrifice of the individualistic clinging to a separation from the All. The sacrifice of the separate ego is the *sine qua non* of this perception.

The perception of a sage is holistic in the sense that what is seen is seen both in its oneness with all-there-is and in its uniqueness. The uniqueness is there—even Krishna could not replace a single child—but it is seen as embedded in the whole. The same Divine energy is manifested in myriad forms and at different levels of consciousness and being, much as the same light from the Sun is reflected uniquely by each leaf and each drop of water, forming quite wondrous and varied patterns.

YOGA AS SCIENCE

The essential science that is needed according to this perspective is Yoga, which is the science (and technology) for bringing about unitary insight. The nature of Yoga and its relationship to Western science are treated elsewhere in this volume in chapter 3 "Perception in Yoga and Physics" and chapter 5 "Yoga and Knowledge."

Yoga knowledge is primarily oriented towards the transformation of a person's consciousness from the ordinary to the unitary, so that nature, which includes us, reveals itself in its wholeness and integrity, without violence and exploitation. Yoga establishes the right internal order, which is the first principle of true ecology. One who truly knows understands that to know is to love. And in this dance of love we know and we are known. In that state, we see the oneness of all there is—and yet the uniqueness of each thing.

From a spiritual perspective—such as the one elaborated above in the context of India—modern science is a product of a limited consciousness. It is useful and even true in its own domain, but it is imperative that our tendencies toward control, manipulation, and violence—which science reflects and supports—be kept in check by the unitive understanding of human beings with respect to other beings at all levels, as well as with the whole of nature, subtle and gross. This control is possible only when the leaders, scientists, and writers are willing to submit themselves to spiritual disciplines by which alone compassion and wisdom can be cultivated.

If you and I are not seen deep down as one, we will always struggle for supremacy over one another. When the angels and the beasts speak of us, what do they say we have wrought?

PERCEPTION IN YOGA AND PHYSICS

In spite of our wish to reconcile science and mysticism, we are very far even from having clear questions to raise about the two approaches to reality. We wish these disciplines to be reconciled because they both appear to us to be significant and profound manifestations of the human psyche, and we imagine that somehow in modern times we have found a reconciliation. Yet we tend not to be very clear as to whether, in talking about science, we are thinking of the scientific revolution of 1905, when Einstein put forth his theories, or of quantum mechanics, which was developed in the 1920s, or of holography of the 1960s, or of theoretical developments in the understanding of chaos or dissipative structures.

Both Yoga, which is an expression of mysticism, and physics are interested in objective knowledge. However, the two "knowledges" are different from each other, and many of their differences relate to the nature of perception in the two disciplines. We need to be aware of these differences if we are to avoid settling for an easy integration or a superficial reconciliation. Nothing is more misleading than to imagine that there is peace when there is no peace. The illusion that we have already found what we need will prevent us from seeking further.

At every stage in the history of science, some scientists have thought, as some do today, that they have the right answers. Furthermore, they think that they know and are talking about precisely the same things that the great mystics and sages of the past have spoken about. For example, it is not generally known that Newton, whose mechanics are now considered a heartless *bête noir* by all those who think that contemporary physics is mystically inclined but the classical one was not, self-consciously attempted to model himself after Chaldean mystic-scientists. He was convinced that he was not saying anything that had not been known to the wise ones of the ancient world. He said that even his inverse square law of gravitational attraction was known to Pythagoras and Moses, among others, and that he was merely expressing it in a form more understandable in his time (Ravindra, "Newton").

But if the insights and the answers of the ancient sages do not appeal to us, then we say that now we have the right answers and that the earlier people were mistaken. Every age believes that its scientific theories have the correct answers or will soon have them. Still, we remain inwardly fragmented and in sorrow.

The sages of the Vedas and Upanishads and the biblical prophets lived thousands of years ago, but we still find much in common with them across the ages and the geographic distances. Our scientific pronouncements, on the other hand, are likely to change in ten years or a hundred years or a thousand years. They are almost certain to change in another three or four thousand years, which is the length of time since the sages and the prophets spoke. So, one wonders about this easy equation of something that is very transient with something that we ourselves say has not changed and will not change because it is eternal and timeless.

Six thousand years from now the sages of the Vedas and other mystical sages will still say the same things, whereas we can be certain that physicists of the future will say different things. Unless we imagine that, in our steadily progressive science, we scientists are saying today the same things as the Buddha or Lao-tzu—with the implication that in the next hundred years we will be able to say yet wiser things—then we must recognize the differences between what the scientists and the mystics say and seek.

It is obvious that observations and perceptions play a very great role in scientific knowledge. In fact, if anything, one might say that one of the great hallmarks of the scientific revolution of the sixteenth and seventeenth centuries was the insistence by natural philosophers that observations were necessary to come to truth and that one could not just sit down and think to arrive at truth. The same is true in Yoga: The whole point of Yoga is to come to clear and direct perceptions. Thus the nature of perception is central to understand both physics and Yoga.

As we are comparing physics and Yoga, we must be clear about what is meant by "Yoga." A story in the Chhandogya Upanishad conveys the meaning of Yoga. A famous sage had a very bright son called Shvetaketu. When the boy came of age, his father said to him, "Son, in our family we have been Brahmins not only in name but because we have been seekers of Brahman. We have been called Brahmins because we have been ardent seekers of the Vastness. You must go and seek knowledge of Brahman."

So Shvetaketu left home to seek knowledge of Brahman, and he studied, it is said, for twelve years. When he returned, having mastered all the sciences, he was very learned, very arrogant, and very self-assured. He told his father about all his learning. His father listened to him and asked him questions and determined that his son was indeed very learned about many matters. Then the father said, "Shvetaketu, you are so learned and so wise and so arrogant, but did you learn that teaching by which the unhearable becomes heard and by which the unseeable becomes seen?" One can guess the answer Shvetaketu gave; he had not been taught to hear the unhearable and he had not heard of such a teaching. If he had, he would not have been so arrogant. Then Shvetaketu asked his father, who had knowledge of an altogether different order of reality, for instruction.

For present purposes, Yoga is that teaching by which the unhearable becomes heard and the unseen becomes seen. This sense of Yoga does not refer to a specific path, but to any spiritual path by which an internal integration takes place so that one can access an altogether different, more subtle and more comprehensive order of reality. Literally, etymologically, the word *Yoga* means "integration"; and a Yogi is one who is integrated.

EXPERIMENT AND EXPERIENCE

Any path by which human beings can be made whole and integrated is a form of Yoga. It is important for us to be clear about the distinction between a "spiritual path" and whatever we have come to call "religion." These two things can and, in general, do exist apart from each other. It may even be the case that most of what we call religion is actually an obstruction on a spiritual path. But here I speak only about the spiritual path or the way of Yoga.

Perception is very important in both physics and Yoga. Objective knowledge is sought and empirical verification is important in both disciplines. They are both experimental or experiential and empirical. But let us distinguish the two words "experiment" and "experience." The modern natural sciences are thoroughly experimental in character, but they are almost determinedly contra-experiential. Yet these two words are often used as though they meant the same thing (cf. chapter 4, "Western Science and Technology and the Indian Intellectual Tradition," and chapter 7, "Experience and Experiment," in this volume).

Experiment comes from the Latin word *experimentum*, and *experience* from the Latin word *experientia*. They are both derived from *experiens*, the present participle of *experiri*, which is made up of two parts, *ex-* and *periri*. The second part is connected with the same root from which the word *peril* comes in English. In this context, *ex-* means "thoroughly." So, to try something thoroughly, to put oneself in peril, to risk one's self, to undergo—these are the root meanings of the Latin word *experiens*. Although *experience* and *experiment* are both derived from this word, for nearly three hundred years they have been used in very different contexts.

Experiment is no longer used as a transitive verb; it is used only intransitively, unlike *experience*. For example, I can experience a flower but I cannot experiment a flower. I have to experiment "on" or "with" a flower. One might think that this is just linguistic finesse that doesn't really matter, but it is important that the word *experiment* sets things apart from the one who is involved. One experiments "on" human beings or rats, "with" LSD or flowers. What one experiences is quite different and more immediate. A scientist in his laboratory experiments with things and makes measurements based on those experiments; it is wholly erroneous to say that the scientist experiences those things.

PERSONAL EQUATION

No doubt, in really simple observations, sometimes experimenting and experiencing come close to each other or may even coalesce. But this is not so for practically any observations now made in science, especially in physics. The question of the involvement of personal perceptions in science is a rather complicated question. But scientists try, as assiduously and carefully as they can, to avoid what they call the "personal equation." This avoidance has nothing to do with whether quantum mechanics has reintroduced the observer into the picture, which is quite irrelevant to whether I am feeling angry or happy, whether I have a lover or I don't, whether I am short or tall, whether I am a Buddhist or a Hindu or a Christian. All such considerations are the "personal equation," and are irrelevant to and must be eliminated from experimental observations.

To be sure, historians of science have often pointed out that it is not always easy to be free of such considerations. When one actually looks at some previous scientific work, one can sometimes see that Germans tend to think along certain lines and the English think along different lines. There are national styles of doing science, and there are specific decades and centuries during which specific problems were considered more important in England than in France. A scientist's cultural and personal conditioning naturally affects the style and the direction of the scientist's inquiry. Nevertheless, one must try to eliminate from science what we call the personal equation.

This is an important matter. Often it is said that the effort to eliminate the personal is what makes science international. Or it is claimed that science is intersubjective because individual scientists are not influenced by their subjective emotions. Underlying such claims is a wish for objectivity and also a very correct perception that most of our ordinary emotional life is contradictory. It is based on "I like this" or "I don't like that" or on fear or pleasure. For the sake of objectivity, it is good not to fall for these subjective ramblings of the heart or mind. There is a right perception underneath all of this, and the attempt in science has been, more particularly since the great scientific revolution of the sixteenth and seventeenth centuries, to be free of these personal wishes and concerns in the process of making scientific observations and forming hypotheses.

But science has thrown out the baby with the bath water. It is a unanimous understanding in all spiritual disciplines (and this is the way I am using the word "Yoga" here, rather than merely for a set of beliefs) that the feelings themselves are an avenue to knowledge and that they are the instruments for the highest form of knowledge. A cleansing or a deepening of these feelings is required so that one can come to objective knowledge through feeling. One of Goethe's very perceptive remarks was that mysticism is a dialectic of feeling. By contrast, one could say that science is a dialectic of reason. All observations and experiments in science are primarily generated by reason and are in the service of reason.

There is an interplay between theory and observation or between conceptions and perceptions in both Yoga and physics. But the interplay enters these disciplines differently. In physics, experimental data, observations, and perceptions are all in the service of theory. They either test theories or generate larger and more comprehensive theories. What we ultimately end up calling scientific knowledge is an ensemble of theories.

On the other hand, theory in Yoga or any spiritual discipline is in the service of perception. It ultimately doesn't matter very much what theory one has. The theory is a device or a trick to quiet the mind or to enlarge the mind. Of course, theory is required in Yoga as well. Along every path one has to study a lot of metaphysical theory. However, if a spiritual discipline remains within that, or if it remains in the service of enhancing further theories, it is merely empty theological talk. Such speculative talk is persuasive enough for us to know that one can be easily caught up in it; all sorts of theological schools and philosophy departments are dedicated to this enterprise.

The usual religious person or an ordinary Yogi or a common person who aspires to be a mystic is as far from the Christ or the Buddha as an ordinary scientist is from Newton or Einstein. We might as well keep our attention on great scientists and sages so that we can understand the deep differences among them by looking at the best practitioners of their respective crafts. What is at issue here? Ultimately the point about the Buddha or the Christ is not that they have a metaphysics or a theory. But the point about Newton and Einstein is exactly that they have a theory. The importance of scientists is due to their theories. Perceptions and conceptions play roles in physics that are quite different from those in Yoga.

Now let us look at the attempt to eliminate the person from the equation. A wish for objectivity is the underlying motive for this. However, the elimination of oneself or one's emotions from scientific observation has far-reaching consequences. Strictly speaking, the nature of the scientist should not affect the observations made. For example, the only requirements relevant to studying physical optics are those available even to someone who is blind (as especially emphasized by the positivist philosophers of the Vienna Circle). We need to ponder this. In physics, the theories or the experiments in optics should be available even to a blind person.

The state or the nature of the scientist is irrelevant to the observations. For example, whether it is the Buddha looking at the path of electrons or whether it is an ordinary person looking at them, even though they may see different things, we must select only the part of their perceptions that is common to both of them. I think this is a way of impoverishing our perceptions. Since the level of consciousness or the state of being of the scientist is irrelevant to the observations, all scientific observations are irrelevant to the level of consciousness of the scientist. Nothing in science would help raise anybody's level of being, at least nothing in science as we know and practice it now.

The metaphysics of modern science has built right into it the axiom that the state of being of scientists is irrelevant to the science they produce. Whether one is good, bad, fearful, hateful, or kind is beside the point in determining one's qualities as a scientist. (We should keep in mind that a majority of all scientists and technologists in the world actually work for the military or for the war machine in one form or another.) The assumption that the level of a person's consciousness or moral preparation is irrelevant to the quality of science that the person does is built into the procedures of science. The complementary obverse of this idea is that whatever we know in science is impotent in changing our level of being.

A very old philosophical debate necessitated this kind of limitation. This debate, which was about the distinction between "primary" and "secondary" qualities, took on a particular importance in the sixteenth and seventeenth centuries in Europe. In gathering knowledge, one cannot take everything into account; certain limitations must be imposed. A question thus arises about which qualities or which properties of matter are to be considered fundamental to reality and which are relatively superficial.

Another way of putting it is: "In what basic terms should we attempt to explain the whole of nature?"

During the sixteenth and seventeenth centuries, decisions were made about this question, sometimes self-consciously, sometimes not. Those properties that could be mathematically and quantitatively determined, such as "mass," "size," and "proportion," were considered primary. Later on, "charge" was also added to this list. But aspects of color, taste, smell, and touch were not considered primary; they were regarded as subjective qualities, identified as secondary. Physicists can talk at length about their methods to determine the primary properties; although there may be uncertainties, within the limits of those uncertainties, there are procedures and ways to determine what the mass of an electron is.

But if we were to ask what the color of an electron is, the question sounds a little ludicrous, although some physicists do have metaphorical fun with that kind of thing. If we ask what the taste of an electron is, that is too subjective; yet mass and charge constitute primary reality even though neither can be sensed directly by anybody, for they are very abstract concepts. If one asks what the purpose of an electron is, one is out of the scientific arena altogether.

There are only certain properties of matter that are considered fundamental. Aspects like color can be explained in terms of other entities that are ultimately related with mass and charge; for example, they may be explained in terms of vibrations of matter or of an electric field. Obviously, some lucky guesses were made in the sixteenth and seventeenth centuries; much of physics has been based on these with remarkable success. Yet this distinction between primary and secondary qualities, which made color subjective and not a fundamental constituent of reality, used to bother Goethe very much; it was an important point in his profound (but completely ignored) critique of Newton.

PERCEPTIONS IN YOGA AND SCIENCE

Both science and Yoga proceed from the assumption that reality as revealed by our ordinary senses is not quite what in truth is real—it is not the real reality. Both claim that the truth behind appearances cannot be seen with unaided or unrefined perception. A physicist tries to enhance the sensitivity of the organs of perception through the development of scientific instruments. This enhancement of the organs of perception is largely quantitative. I look at an object with the eyes I have; then with a microscope I can see smaller objects, or with a telescope, far-away objects, but I still look at them in exactly the same way; my valuation of them does not change.

On the other hand, the direction in Yoga is much as the great visionary William Blake spoke of it, as a need to cleanse one's organs of perception. Such a cleansing is qualitative; the perception of the same reality before and after cleansing has a different quality and significance. Every spiritual discipline subjects the student to a great deal of personal suffering, because in a spiritual discipline the sculptor, the chisel, and the stone are the same—they are all parts of the self. One is trying to sculpt something out of the given stone and with means that are really in oneself, although teachers can help.

In a spiritual discipline, a cleansing of the internal organs of perception is required. Whenever one becomes aware of the muddiness of one's perceptions, something like the Dark Night of the Soul ensues, causing much suffering to the person experiencing it. The elimination of feelings because they are unreliable is not suggested, but rather, with the recognition that uneducated feelings are unreliable, one sees the need to undertake a discipline of training the feelings so that one can come to those that are more reliable and objective.

In physics we externalize our perceptions, even of those things that are inside us. A computer can perform many of the functions of the ordinary organs of perception. For example, in a scientific experiment, it may be possible for us, given enough research grants, to set up a mechanism so that the scientists can go home to lunch and the data will be there when they come back. In many scientific experiments, the actual presence or participation of human scientists is not necessary for the collection of data.

Of course, scientists are necessary to set up the experiment, to interpret the data, and to apply the results; so scientists are still needed. However, the actual scientific perceptions, precisely where there is a direct contact with reality, whether one is measuring the scattering of electrons, studying the heartbeat of a fetus in the uterus, or investigating the reactions of rats towards certain kinds of controlled stimuli, do not need real, live human beings. Perceiving can be done without the presence of the scientists as far as the collection of data is concerned. That is to say, perceptions can be completely externalized, and one's organs of perception can be taken outside and quantitatively extended.

On the other hand, such externalization of perception is not the case in Yoga, where, if anything, a complete and total internalization takes place. Both science and Yoga, however, assert that our ordinary organs of perception, as they are, are not quite adequate for perceiving reality.

In Yoga, there is a recognition or an assumption that, "as one is, so one sees." This is not at all true in science, where only those perceptions are admitted for which it is irrelevant what kind of person one is. A great sundering or separation between knowing and being is at issue here; the level of being or state of consciousness of a person is irrelevant for producing scientific knowledge, but critically relevant for Yoga.

What is the point or purpose of the knowledge involved in science and in Yoga? Why are we so excited about scientific knowledge? Supposing we knew all about Mars, what would that change? Albert Camus remarked, in his *Myth of Sisyphus*, that whether the moon goes around the earth or the earth goes around the moon is quite irrelevant in life. As a young physicist, I was much bothered by this and wondered about this strange kind of philosophy. But why *are* we so interested in scientific knowledge?

KNOWING AND BEING

If we look at the uses to which scientific knowledge is generally put, we see a very strong wish for control and manipulation of whatever we study. Of course, many things are not subject to control, as least not easily. They may be too distant, as most things in astronomy are. Still the methods and procedures that have been developed are based on a wish for control. This was classically expressed by Francis Bacon, the patron saint of the Royal Society of London, who said that human beings should study nature in order to control it and utilize it for the betterment of the estate of humanity.

The scientific motivation by a wish for control and manipulation is quite different from the point of view taken in Yoga, except for a recent emphasis in some scientific circles interested in the study of consciousness. However, whenever we approach the study of consciousness with our present scientific attitude, we are always going to ask how we can control it and how we can use it. When this attitude comes into psychology, particularly in the transition zone between the psyche and the spirit (cf. chapter 9, "To the Dancer Belongs the Universe" in this volume), it always represents what used to be called "demonic" tendencies.

If we proceed with the present scientific attitude to a study of the spirit, what we are going to be concerned with, even if we don't actually formulate it as such, is how we can appropriate the spirit for our purposes and for our use. So we ask, how can we use meditation to get ahead in business, to be better lovers, or to be more successful? The attitude of a Yogi would be, not "How can I appropriate the spirit for my use?" but "How can I be appropriated by the spirit for its use?" In Yoga there is a fundamentally different attitude to the purpose and value of knowledge from that of science. Different kinds and means of perception are connected with these different approaches.

What is the purpose of knowledge? In Yoga the point of knowledge really is the ending of knowledge. This is what the word *vedānta* literally means: "the end of knowledge." When we realize the essential unknowability of the Vastness *(Brahman)* of which we are a part, then we can become quiet in mind and heart and participate in this Vastness. In that sense, one who knows Brahman becomes Brahman. We cannot know it, apart from it. The central problem is of being, not of knowing. In Yoga, knowing serves being, and ultimately it is a self-destructive art. After it has served its function, it is transcended. An old metaphor says that knowledge is like a ladder one uses to go up; once one is up, it is stupid to go on carrying the ladder. Science, however, has a fundamentally different metaphysics, and part of its metaphysics assumes that being is not at all relevant to knowledge, so certainly there is no reason to go beyond knowledge.

Because the point of Yoga is to end knowledge, the aim of a Yogi is to end clinging to the separateness of the observer from the observed. As the Christian scriptures (John 12.25) say, it is only when we can leave our self behind that we can follow Christ. The little self is made up of all this knowing: of the past, present, and future; of fears and pleasures; of likes and dislikes. On the path of Yoga, these "knowings" of the little self have to be discarded for the greater self to emerge, just as a sculptor chisels away the unnecessary parts a stone to help the sculpture to emerge.

Through Yoga, right order emerges, as does the end of knowledge, the end of isolated individuality, the end of separation, and the end of time. According to Patañjali, the celebrated author of the *Yoga Sūtra*, the greatest illusion is *asmitā*. It is difficult to render this word into English, but it is something like "I-am-this-ness," a state of egotism. He went on to define this condition (which was similarly described by William Blake) as the misperception that what might be seen is limited to what the organs of sight can see. Thus, the point of Yoga really is to go beneath, behind, or beyond our ordinary organs of perception. As the Upanishads say, one who does not see that whatever is inside is also outside is truly deluded. Since to assume that the seer is constrained by the apparatus of seeing is a fundamental error, a Yogi purifies and integrates the perceptions so that what is seen is not as much seen with the eyes as through the eyes.

A dialogue by the German mystic, Jakob Böhme, is relevant here:

Disciple: Oh, how may I arrive at the unity of will, and how to come into the unity of vision?

Master: Mark now what I say; the Right Eye looks in you into eternity. The Left Eye looks backward in you into time. If now you suffer yourself to be always looking into nature, and the things of time, it will be impossible for you ever to arrive at the unity you wish for. Remember this; and be on your guard. Give not your mind leave to enter in, nor to fill itself with, that which is without you; neither look backward upon yourself. Let not your Left Eye deceive you, by making continually one representation after another, and stirring up thereby an earnest longing in the self-propriety; but let your Right Eye command back this Left. . . . And only bringing the Eye of Time into Eye of Eternity . . . and descending through the Light of God into the Light of Nature . . . will you arrive at the Unity of Vision or Uniformity of Will.

These days esoteric knowledge, from within this culture as well as from other cultures far away in space and time, is readily available in any bookstore, easily and promiscuously accessible. This free availability of the esoteric is partly due to our scientific mentality, which gives no importance to the distinctions between levels of being or between levels of knowledge. In such circumstances, where are our guardians? What are our safeguards?

There is a traditional notion, not only in India but also in every classical tradition of which I am aware, that truth is something for which one has to be prepared in order to understand. Not only *understand;* one has to be prepared to *withstand* it as well, because truth can be devastating. How are we preparing ourselves for a profound esoteric knowledge so that we can not only understand it but also withstand it? What preparation do our intellectual or political leaders have so that they won't misuse this knowledge? How is this esoteric knowledge going to transform our being if we regard it just as we regard scientific knowledge?

To imagine that the science of today is equivalent to ancient esoteric knowledge, presumably because of some superficial similarities in some expressions, is an indication of a complete ignorance of the methods and aims of ancient spiritual traditions. Implicit in these sentimental assertions of similarity and equivalence of modern science and esoteric knowledge is a naive and arrogant assumption that tomorrow, or in the next decade or the next century or surely by the next millennium, our science will far surpass the knowledge of the ancient mystics, sages, and prophets. From a spiritual and traditional point of view, such assertions are not merely innocently ignorant, but dangerous and soporific; they are ways of nullifying the possibility of esoteric knowledge for bringing human beings into a state of wakefulness, to their proper place in the cosmos, to their responsibility in the maintenance of right inner and outer order, and to their real possibilities.

It is easy for us, individually and culturally, to be lulled back to sleep, away from a disquieting moment of waking up and seeing, into a dream in which we plan the conquest of inner space and of consciousness and in which we imagine ourselves at the same level of understanding as the greatest of past sages, while remaining content with superficial appearances. By our refusal to be woken up by esoteric knowledge and by our wish to master it for our own egoistic purposes, we prevent this knowledge from working in us to transform our being, to bring us to the end of that knowledge concerned with acquisition and control, to help us be free of ourselves, and to bring us to a stillness in which we can be aware of our essential unknowing and not be paralyzed into inaction or frightened into the lap of the deceptive security of explanations. Above all, we need right discrimination in order to see our situation clearly and enough strength to bear the demands of transformation.

An Indian story is relevant to the perception of esoteric knowledge: Once there was a great sage called Bhagiratha. He made great efforts and undertook spiritual austerities; so he was blessed by being granted whatever boon he asked for. Because he had seen human beings parched for the life-giving waters of real knowledge, he asked the gods to let the river Ganga, which flowed in heaven, descend to the earth. The boon was granted; but the gods feared that since the river Ganga (which we might take here as esoteric knowledge) flowed only in heaven, if it were to descend to the earth, the planet (or ourselves as our ordinary body-mind), not being prepared to receive the shock of Ganga's descent, would be shattered. Shiva, the Lord of the Yogis, therefore agreed to take the impact of the descent of the river on his head. From his head, the water came down to the earth in seven life-giving streams. Of all the gods, Shiva is the guardian deity of transformation. He alone is able to overcome the sleep of illusion and subdue the force of desire with the fire of the discriminative vision of his third eye.

Who among us will invoke Shiva and act on his behalf in the present moment of deep crisis and radical opportunity?

WESTERN SCIENCE AND TECHNOLOGY AND THE INDIAN INTELLECTUAL TRADITION

Every major culture develops, over a period of time, an internal integrity. Its major manifestations—arts, religions, philosophies, and science-technology—are closely interrelated. It is a mark of the vitality of the intellectual tradition of a country that these various manifestations interact, nourishing and challenging one another. Tensions and contradictions among them can be very creative and can lead to a synthesis at a higher level. On the other hand, because of a lack of fearless effort in resolving such contradictions, a culture can be satisfied with superficial reconciliation.

One important cultural contradiction in present-day India relates to modern science and technology. Both intellectuals and well-intentioned laymen in India tend to imagine that modern science and technology do not contradict the Indian spiritual-intellectual tradition. It has even been suggested that the Indian tradition, rightly understood, will naturally lead to modern science. These sentiments seem to be based more on a vague feeling that all good things are inherently harmonious than on any close analysis of the situation.

We certainly hope that modern science and ancient spiritual traditions can be integrated into some higher synthesis. Indeed, such a task is the most important one to be undertaken by contemporary intellectuals, for on such a synthesis depends both the global survival of humanity and the creation of an environment that is right for future generations, both physically and metaphysically. This, however, is a challenge that cannot be met easily. Perhaps the intellectual effort of a whole generation will be needed for the task. There are some signs now in the Western world, and in particular in the United States, but hardly any in India, that this task is beginning to be undertaken on several fronts with a vigorous quality of thought and a lack of sentimentalism. A necessary step is to understand clearly the essential nature of modern science and technology.

Modern science and technology everywhere—East or West—are essentially Western in character. Their fundamental procedures and attitudes were developed in Western Europe during the great scientific revolution of the sixteenth and seventeenth centuries. The rise and the development of modern science are closely linked with the spread of certain humanistic and secular sociopolitical ideas in the West. There are several philosophical presuppositions concerning the nature of reality, of human beings, and of knowledge that underlie modern science and technology; and they all arise from Western religions and philosophy. It is necessary to be aware of these presuppositions, for it is likely that the spread of modern science and technology—whose philosophical attitudes differ from those of ancient and medieval sciences and technologies even in the West and certainly from those in India—will bring with it the same sort of spiritual ruin in India as it has in the West, unless we can bring the requisite understanding and the will for a higher cultural synthesis. Some of these philosophical presuppositions, though by no means all, are discussed below.

EVERYTHING IS ESSENTIALLY DEAD

All scientific inquiry assumes that the objects it is investigating are essentially dead, that is, they have no interiority. They have no consciousness, purpose, or intention of their own, and their entire existence and behavior can be explained by their interactions with outside forces that are themselves purposeless. Therefore, those objects—whether electron, frog, man, or culture—can be completely described in terms of external forces to which they react helplessly.

The reality of Western science, on a small scale or as a whole, may be dynamic but it has no self-initiative. Modern Western cosmology is based completely on physics, which investigates dead matter in motion in reaction to external forces. Reality is seen as internally completely passive: It reacts to forces but it cannot respond. The psychological theory called "stimulus-response" is misnamed and should more properly be called "stimulus-reaction."

The model everywhere in modern science is physics, which bases itself entirely on principles derived from a study of objects that are assumed to be completely inanimate. One may think that the foregoing comment does not apply to biology, which after all deals with living organisms. This is true only in the minimal sense that the objects studied by biology have a property called "reproducibility." They are allowed no more interiority than the dead objects of physics. So monkeys, cats, and frogs have no rights that might mitigate against any sort of experimentation on them. The only relevant fact is that human beings can overpower these animals and therefore subject them to any treatment whatsoever.

Theological and ethical considerations aside, which are in any case notorious for their impotence in the laboratories, there is no scientific principle that would stand in the way of experimentation on the members of a subject race. Also the basic thrust of the entire work in biophysics and biochemistry is to find explanations of "living" organisms in terms of dead objects and purposeless forces, that is, in terms of physical laws.

In an older terminology, one might say that biology deals with animals as if they had no "souls" and were only bodies. This, of course, is an old and standard Christian idea. Only human beings have souls; they are different from other animals precisely in this way. (For that matter, in the past, the question has been raised whether slaves, blacks, or women have souls.) Descartes, who is regarded as the father of modern Western philosophy and who had an enormous influence on modern biology, regarded animals very much in this Christian light and considered them as "engines without will." A human being, on the other hand, for Descartes was an engine with a will.

Modern psychology, as it became progressively more "scientific," naturally eliminated any considerations of interiority, treating human beings only like machines reacting to external stimuli in a predictable manner. Most of experimental and behaviorist psychology is based on the assumption that human beings can, in principle, be completely characterized by their reactions to external forces and that we need not entertain the idea of there being "a ghost in the machine," which we can label as consciousness or soul and which may be said to have an intention or purpose.

There is no principle of scientific epistemology that permits the treatment of human beings as persons rather than as objects. To be sure, other orientations in the field of psychology have arisen in the last few decades, for example, orientations labeled "humanistic psychology" and "existential psychology," but the common charge against them is precisely that they are not sufficiently "scientific."

This attitude also permeates modern scientific medicine, namely that a human being is essentially a physicochemical machine that is somehow alive—a fact itself determined by some external physical characteristics. In this machine, different components (traditionally called "organs") can, in principle, be replaced by "living" or artificial components with similar functions from elsewhere.

In short, a fundamental assumption of modern scientific inquiry is that the whole of reality, on whatever scale we perceive it—as the whole universe, an animal, a tree, or a stone—is a machine. Whether it has any consciousness or not is quite irrelevant to scientific procedures and conclusions; therefore, for simplicity, one might as well proceed on the assumption that there is no consciousness. The whole of nature is assumed to be made up of dead matter in purposeless motion. In fact, nothing whatsoever has any purpose. Neither purpose nor anything equivalent is a scientific category at all. Any suggestion of purpose, in the idea of a "final cause" as held by philosophers before the major scientific revolution of the sixteenth and seventeenth centuries, has been systematically eliminated since then. Now, objects or creatures do not have purposes; they merely have functions.

OTHERNESS OF NATURE

The otherness of nature is an essential presupposition of the scientific attitude, which sees the universe as hostile or at least indifferent—not intentionally but mechanically—to human purposes and aspirations. Therefore, nature needs to be fought and conquered. This view allows humans to exploit nature. The more advanced a society is scientifically and technologically, the more pronounced is its exploitation of nature.

Modern technology is of a piece with modern science in its procedures and attitudes. What distinguishes them is their stance toward the
control of nature. In science, the control of nature is tantamount to understanding nature, and one engages in it for the sport of it, for the pleasure
of overcoming an adversary. In technology, the advantage over nature is
exploited for gratification of human desires, usually in the guise of as-
suaging fears and fulfilling needs.

Utilizing natural resources for the fulfillment of legitimate human
needs has shifted to exploiting nature for the gratification of unbridled
desires. This shift—clearly in the United States and increasingly elsewhere—is made possible by the increased capabilities of science and
technology. It is made easy by the attitude, common to science and technology, of regarding nature as an enemy to be vanquished.

OBJECTIVITY OF REALITY

Closely related with the above two presuppositions is another, according to which "nature" inside us is wholly different from nature outside.
This presupposition is related to Descartes's well-known sharp division between two realms: *res extensa* (realm of extension) and
res cogitans (realm of thinking). The former is the realm of the body; it
is the material domain of nature. The latter is the realm of the soul, which
for Descartes is the same as the mind. Nature is only material and external. What is internal is merely subjective—in the sense of being
personal, private, shifting, and unreliable. Only what is external can be
objective and real.

QUANTIFICATION OF REALITY

Even in the external realm a further division is made between the so-
called primary and secondary qualities. This division is necessitated by
the demand of an unambiguous intersubjective agreement about the external characteristics of an object.

Primary qualities are those characteristics that can be quantified and measured. As Max Planck, the twentieth-century physicist who was the father of quantum mechanics, said, "That which cannot be measured is not real." Things that can be measured are thus divorced from any consideration of the relative quality of attention, clarity of perception, or level of being of any observer.

What is assumed to be primarily real about anything excludes, not only the distortions likely to be introduced by agitated or wishful thinking, but also the more subtle aspects perceivable only by sensitive and refined minds. Reality is thus, by assumption, divested of feelings and sensations requiring cleansed perceptions, such as some artists and mystics have, and is reduced to only those characteristics that can be mechanically quantified, such as size and mass. "Just as the eye was made to see colors, and the ear to hear sounds," wrote Kepler, "so the human mind was made not to understand whatever you please, but quantity" (quoted by Burtt 68).

A philosophical analogue of this quantitative attitude is in Anglo-American analytical philosophy, particularly as it was practiced from the mid-1940s to the mid-1960s. That school, which sought the solution of philosophical problems not in the contemplation of problems, but in the analysis of statements about them, reduced the vast and subtle realm of truth to propositions for which one can prepare "truth tables" determining whether a particular proposition is true or false.

Secondary qualities are all the features of reality with which the arts and religions have been traditionally concerned, such as color, sound, taste, beauty, and purpose. Whatever functions poetry, music, dance, or spiritual disciplines may serve, when it comes to the serious business of truth and knowledge, as understood by modern natural philosophers, all these activities are essentially frivolous. Herein lie the seeds of fragmentation of our sensibilities: Arts and religion cannot lead to "knowledge" and science cannot lead to "values."

The resultant dichotomy between "knowledge" and "faith" or between "reason" and "feeling," particularly apparent in Western culture, tends to be destructive of human wholeness and leads to narrow single vision. If our modern gods of truth and reason admit physics to their temples but not poetry or music or spiritual search, the wisdom of such gods is questionable. It may well be, as William Blake said, that "Reason and Newton they are quite two things."

REALITY IS A MENTAL CONSTRUCT

Science assumes an abstract and purely rational construct underlying perceived reality. So what is experienced is called "appearance," and the mental construct is labeled "reality." The scientific pursuit is to speculate about the imagined reality and to put these speculations to experimental tests, which involve only certain limited perceptions. The so-called objective reality of scientific concern is in fact a conjecture—perhaps one of many that are possible. However—and this is where the importance and glory of science lie—these subjective projections are confirmed or falsified by intersubjective experimental procedures.

Nevertheless, testing procedures are not wholly independent of the theoretical framework they test. As scientific experiments become more elaborate, whether an observation confirms a given conjecture is increasingly a matter of interpretation. It is not possible to make a scientific observation without a prior theory, as has been emphasized by Karl Popper. In science, any theory is better than no theory. In order to get going, scientists are happy to have partial, incomplete, or wrong theories rather than wait for a correct one; until a new theory is available, an old one is not abandoned, however many problems it may have.

Theorizing is fundamental to scientific activity; what scientists subject to experimental observations is not nature, but their conjectures about nature. The scientific revolution marks a shift not only from experience to experiment (cf. chapter 7, "Experience and Experiment" in this volume) but also from seeking certain truth to theorizing about probable truths. In science, reality is theory.

The centrality of theory is true for all sciences, not physics alone. Every experimental science is first of all a theoretical science, although its theoretical system may be more or less explicit. Here is an example from Sigmund Freud (*General Introduction* 60, emphasis added): "Our purpose is not merely to describe and classify phenomena but to conceive them as brought about by the play of forces in the mind, as expressions of tendencies striving towards a goal, which work together or against one another. In this conception, the trends we merely *infer* are more prominent than the phenomena we *perceive*."

Reality discovered through science is not necessarily something that is given, which we try to perceive more and more clearly and comprehensively by deepening or cleansing our perceptions, as one attempts, for example, in Yoga. It is instead something postulated on the basis of data gathered through our ordinary perceptions, or perceptions that have been quantitatively extended through scientific instruments, but not qualitatively transformed. The reality of science is not substantial, available to an immediate experience of anybody whosoever; it is conjectural and inferential.

Scientific knowledge is not of "minute particulars" that can be directly and immediately apprehended. The phrase "minute particulars" is William Blake's. It does not imply any restriction of scale; a "minute particular" could be a whole constellation of stars, the earth, a person, or a tree. To know something as a minute particular is to know it in its concrete uniqueness—which need not be material, but could be supersensuous. The idea is similar to the Indian notion that everything—tree, river, earth—has an indwelling spirit *(abhimāni devat)* presiding over it. Scientific knowledge, on the contrary, leads away from immediacy and the attendant certainty to yield abstract generalizations forever subject to reasoning and change.

FABRIC OF REALITY

Time is primarily linear and uniform, space is essentially isotropic, and energy is basically of one quality. Energy can be more or less in quantity but not subtler or grosser in quality. It can in principle be converted from one form to another. These assumptions, particularly about the linearity and uniformity of time, become problematic when considering questions relating to the origin of the entire universe. It is a consequence of these assumptions that the laws of physics are applicable for all time and throughout all space. Also, the laws of conservation of energy, momentum, and angular momentum are intimately connected with the assumed symmetrical properties of space and time.

In ancient and medieval science, different planets were considered to be made up of different types of matter, subject to different laws because they occupied different regions of space and were made for different purposes. According to modern science, the place and function (which is a mechanical replacement for the idea of purpose) of a thing are not inherent to it but are accidental. Therefore, nothing essential or primarily real in the object can depend on its place or function. According to earlier ideas, the earth—with the human beings on it—was situated in a specific place suitable for an intentional interplay of purposive energies. Now, since intention and purpose are not parts of natural philosophy, no place has any special importance with respect to anything. The earth happens to be where it is by chance, following a concatenation of mechanical causes.

Consistent with the presuppositions mentioned earlier, particularly in the section on the "Objectivity of Reality," the time, space, and energy of natural philosophy are all only objectively (that is, externally) real. They are completely independent of the level or the state of the perceiving consciousness, and they cannot in principle be affected by consciousness.

If a miracle takes place that cannot be explained away as a trick, in which "mind" affects objective reality (that is, external time, space, and energy as measured by clocks and sticks), the attitude of modern science is either to ignore it or to regard it as contrary to natural laws or even as supernatural, rather than to admit that our present view of nature is a very limited one. St. Augustine, on the other hand, in harmony with the common traditional Indian view on these matters, makes a useful distinction when he says that we must not regard wonders and signs as "contrary to nature" but "contrary to what is known of nature" (*de Civitate Dei* 21.8).

MATTER PRECEDES INTELLIGENCE

A nearly universal traditional belief holds that causes are at a higher level of subtlety and intelligence than their effects. This idea is clearly enunciated in the philosophical school called Sānkhya, in which grosser manifestations emerge from subtler ones, and ultimately from the unmanifest *(avyakta)*. From this perspective, spirit precedes mind, which in turn precedes matter. In the natural philosophy of the six-teenth and seventeenth centuries in Europe, causes were taken to be at the same level as effects. In physics, the fundamental notion of causality is that, when we say state A of matter causes state B, we mean only that state A changes into state B under specific conditions and subject to physi-cal laws. There is no suggestion whatever that states A and B are at different levels.

In the nineteenth-century theory of evolution of scientific biology, causes are taken to be at a lower level than their effects. Less intelligent organisms precede and give rise to more intelligent animals. Matter pre-cedes all forms of intelligence, which is taken to be a manifestation of a complex organization of matter. Complex material organization and the consequent higher intelligence may be completely accidental or partly a reaction to external environmental pressures. What is important from a scientific point of view is that everything, including apparently inner at-tributes accompanying intelligence, must be explained in terms of external forces and matter. The evolution of a species, for example, has to be ex-plained in terms of environmental adaptation or some other mechanism external to the species, rather than, say, as the evolutionary thrust of con-sciousness needing more complex organisms for manifestation.

WESTERN PRESUPPOSITIONS AND INDIAN TRADITION

All of these philosophical presuppositions are radically at odds with the corresponding assumptions in the Indian tradition. To be sure, great poets and spiritual seekers in the Western tradition (Goethe, Blake, Wordsworth, Yeats, Eliot) have been uneasy with the philosophical and cultural implications of modern science and technology, and much of the contemporary spiritual malaise of the West is intimately linked with their triumph. Here and there, one or another of these assumptions is being challenged in one particular science or another. However, their hegemony is clear from the fact that modern cosmology, which is supposed to be a study of all there is, has become a branch of physics, which deals with dead matter in motion.

One may be tempted to think that the major scientific changes in the twentieth century have affected the foregoing assumptions. This is not the case. Nevertheless, the fact that many people think it is so has helped to prepare an intellectual climate in which a radical reevaluation of science becomes easier. There are some signs of change. The world is in the midst of a great metaphysical revolution that will shake the foundations of all human thinking. This revolution, which does not yet seem to have engaged the intellectuals in India, is calling into question all our established notions of space, time, materiality, causality, and mind. An alternative and a much more comprehensive science than the present one is in the making.

Traditional Eastern spiritual disciplines and philosophies may provide some necessary elements for the emerging alternative philosophy of nature on a global scale if they are cleansed of some extraneous religious accretions. If science and technology in India had had an internal, organic growth, rather than a surgical transplant from elsewhere, as was the case, it is likely that Indian science would be as different from Western science as Indian music is from Western music. There would no doubt be some quite basic similarities, but there would be differences in their essential aspirations. Furthermore, this alternative science and technology would have been more integrated with the rest of the Indian culture.

Whether this Indian science and technology would be adequate for the needs and aspirations of the emerging global culture is an open question. Nevertheless, it is important for India to be free of the unhealthy epistemological imperialism of the West, more pernicious because of its unrecognized character. India does not need to go back to ancient times any more than the West stayed ancient. But history forced an alien development of mind on India without a corresponding change of heart.

The Indian situation is now, however, quite different from that of Europe in the sixteenth and seventeenth centuries, largely because of the introduction of Western science and technology. The major difference is that Indians, unlike Westerners then or now, have to take into account two cultures: their own history, philosophy, science, and religion and also Western history, philosophy, science, and technology. India will ignore the West at her own peril; but if India ignores her own soul, there will be nothing left that needs guarding from any peril.

True to the spirit of her own culture, India cannot depend ultimately on any institutional or technological blueprints. India's future depends on the depth of understanding and the greatness of being of her intellectual leaders. *Buddhi* has an intelligence greater than that of *manas* alone and includes feeling as much as reason. Furthermore a fundamental assumption in the Indian tradition is that to come to great truth one must have a great being. Only those people can truly help in the proper growth of culture—which must be from the inside outward—who are reasonably conversant with Western thought, science, and technology but also who are not overwhelmed by Western culture into a state in which no alternatives are seen.

Nor must Indian intellectuals be indifferent or hostile to Western values and ideas simply because they are alien. The West, like India, has a ray of the limitless truth. The rays are different, perhaps with complementary colors, needing scope for enlargement and expression. The Indian tradition has always believed that truth can be approached in many ways; still one has to find and devote oneself, both on the individual and the cultural scale, to one's own distinctive way. It is only by being authentically ourselves that we can understand the general human situation and contribute to global welfare.

Thus the intellectual leaders in India will have to be deeply in touch with the Indian tradition, aware of its distinctive mission, and in love with it, not for its own sake, but for the sake of the Truth, which is no more Indian than Western. For India to ignore her own essential depth would be to block out one luminous emanation of the universal Sun. That Sun is no mere material ball of fire; it is in truth one of the *Ādityas* (the sacred planetary gods), born from the union of *Aditi* (literally "unlimited," also an ancient goddess of space) and *Kashyapa* (literally "vision," also an ancient sage), constantly dispersing the *Daityas* (demons, the complements of the divine Ādityas), who by contrast are born from a vision that is limited (*Diti*, "limited," also an ancient goddess of earthly phenomena, the complement of Aditi).

YOGA AND KNOWLEDGE

The theory and practice of Yoga originate from above, that is to say, from the vision of the highest possible state of consciousness. It is not something that has been forged or devised from below, or that can even be understood by the human mind, however intelligent such a mind may be. Yoga is a suprahuman *(apaurusheya)* revelation; it is from the realm of the gods. Mythologically, it is said that the Great God Shiva taught Yoga to his beloved Parvati for the sake of humankind. It cannot be validated or refuted by human reasoning; on the contrary, the relative sanity or health of a mind is measured by the extent to which it accords with the sayings of the accomplished sages, who have been transformed by the practice of Yoga. It is a vision by the "third eye," compared with which, our two usual eyes see only shadows.

In spite of the revelatory nature of Yoga, it requires no mere faith, and certainly nothing opposed to knowledge. What it in fact requires is the utmost exertion of the whole of the human being—mind, heart, and body—for a practice that leads to a total transformation of being, a change not less than that of a species mutation. Thus, Yoga not only brings the vision from the third eye of Shiva and of the sages for us to receive, but also aims at helping us develop and open the third eye in ourselves so that we may be of like spiritual vision with Shiva and the sages. This is conveyed by the etymology of the word *Yoga:* It is derived from the root *yuj,* meaning "to yoke, unite, harness." When the human body-mind is harnessed to the Spirit *(Purusha, Atman, Brahman),* which is as much within a human being as outside, the person is in Yoga.

THE AIM OF YOGA

Yoga is at once religion, science, and art, as it is concerned with being *(sat)*, knowing *(jñāna)* and doing *(karma)*. The aim of Yoga, however, is beyond these three, as well as beyond any opposites that they imply (Ravindra, "Is Religion Psychotherapy?"). Yoga aims at *moksha*, which is unconditioned and uncaused freedom. This state of freedom is, by its very nature, beyond the dualities of being-nonbeing, knowledge-ignorance, and activity-passivity. The way to *moksha* is Yoga, which serves as a path or a discipline toward integration.

Achieving the aim of Yoga requires the transformation of a human being from a natural and actual form to a perfect and real form. The *prakrita* (literally, "natural, vulgar, unrefined") state is one in which a person compulsively acts in reaction to the forces of *prakriti* ("nature, causality, materiality"), which are active both outside and inside a person. Ordinarily, a person is a slave of the mechanical forces of nature and all actions are determined by the law of karma, the law of action and reaction. Through Yoga, however, one can become *samskrita* (literally, "well-formed, cultured, refined"), and thus no longer be wholly at the mercy of natural forces and inclinations.

The procedure of Yoga corresponds to the root meaning of the word *education:* It helps draw out what in fact already is in us but was not perceivable in the unpolished form. The progressive bringing out of the real person *(purusha)* in an aspirant is much like the releasing of a figure from an unshaped stone. The undertaking of Yoga concerns the entire person, resulting in a reshaping of mind, body, and emotions—in short, in a *new birth*. Unlike sculpture, the remolding involved in Yoga is essentially from the inside out, for the Yogi is the artist, the stone, and the tools. But a person does not create the state of freedom; if one is properly prepared and does not insist on possessing and controlling everything, one can allow to surface, and to be possessed by, what is deep within.

The analogy between Yoga and sculpting should not be misunderstood as suggesting that Yoga leads to a rugged individualism in which individuals are the makers of their own destiny. The freedom a Yogi aspires to is less a freedom *for* the self than a freedom *from* the self. From a strict metaphysical point of view, a Yogi cannot be said to be the artist of his or her own life; the real initiative belongs only to *Brahman*, lodged in the heart of everyone. A person does not create a state of freedom; but with a proper preparation and without an insistence on possessing and controlling everything, an individual can let surface, and can be possessed by, what is deep within.

THE BODY AND THE EMBODIED

Yoga begins from a recognition of the human situation. Human beings are bound by the laws of process, and they suffer as a consequence of this bondage. Yoga proceeds by a focus on knowledge of the self. Self-knowledge may be said to be both the essential method and the essential goal of Yoga. However, self-knowledge is a relative matter. It depends not only on the depth and clarity of insight, but also on what is seen as the "self" to be known. A progressive change from the identification of the self as the body (including the heart and the mind) to the identification of the self as inhabiting the body is the most crucial development in Yoga. Ancient and modern Indian languages reflect this perspective in the expressions they use to describe a person's death: In contrast to the usual English expression of *giving up the ghost*, one *gives up the body*. It is not the body that has the spirit, but the spirit that has the body. The Yogi identifies the person less with the *body* and more with the *embodied*.

The identification of the person in oneself with something other than the body-mind and the attendant freedom from the body-mind is possible only through a proper functioning and restructuring of the body and the mind. The Sanskrit word *sharīra* is useful in order to steer clear of the modern Western philosophic dilemma called the "mind-body" problem. Although *sharīra* is usually translated as "body," it means the whole psychosomatic complex of body, mind, and heart. *Sharīra* has the same import as *flesh* in the Gospel of Saint John, for example in John 1.14, where it is said, "The Word became flesh and dwelt in us" (Ravindra, *Christ the Yogi*). The important point, both in the Indian context and in John, is that the spiritual element, called *Purusha*, *Atman*, or *Logos* ("Word"), is above the whole of the psychosomatic complex of a human being, and is not to be identified with mind, which is a part of *sharīra* or the "flesh."

Sharīra is both the instrument of transformation as well as the mirror indicating it. Knowing the way a person sits, walks, feels, and thinks can help in knowing the relatively "realer" self; the knowing of this self is then reflected in the way a person sits, walks, feels, and thinks. *Sharīra*, which is miniaturized or individualized *prakriti,* is the medium necessary for the completion and manifestation of the inner spiritual being, which itself can be understood as individualized *Brahman* (literally, "the Vastness"), whose body is the whole of the cosmos, subtle as well as gross.

There is a correspondence between the microcosmos, which is a human being, and the macrocosmos or universe. The more developed a person is, the more that person corresponds to the deeper and more subtle aspects of the cosmos; only a fully developed human being *(mahāpurusha)* mirrors the entire creation. To view the *sharīra* or the world as a hindrance rather than an opportunity is akin to regarding the rough stone as an obstruction to the finished statue.

Sharīra is the substance from which each one of us makes a work of art, according to our ability to respond to the inner urge and initiative. This substance belongs to *prakriti* and includes what are ordinarily called psychic, organic, and inorganic processes. The view that mind and body follow the same laws, or the fact that the psychic, organic, and inorganic substances are treated alike, does not lead to the sort of reductionism associated with the modern scientific mentality, in which the ideal is to describe all of nature ultimately in terms of dead matter in motion reacting to purposeless forces. *Prakriti*, although following strict causality, is alive and purposeful, and every existence, even a stone, has a psyche and purpose. From a traditional perspective, creation is understood to be from above downward; in contradistinction to the view of modern scientific cosmology that matter precedes mind.

SEEING THROUGH THE ORGANS OF PERCEPTION

Although there are many kinds of Yogas, such as *karma Yoga* (integration through action), *bhakti Yoga* (union through love), *jñāna Yoga* (yoking through knowledge), and others, the Indian tradition has in general maintained that there is only one central Yoga, with one central aim of harnessing the entire body-mind to the purposes of the spirit. Different Yogas arise because of the varying emphases on methods and procedures adopted by different teachers and schools.

The most authoritative text of Yoga is the *Yoga Sūtras*, which consists of aphorisms of Yoga compiled by Patañjali sometime between the second century B.C.E. and the fourth century C.E. from material already familiar to the gurus (teachers) of Indian spirituality. It is clearly stated by Patañjali that clear seeing and knowing are functions of *purusha* (the inner person) and not of the mind.

The mind is confined to the modes of judgment, comparison, discursive knowledge, association, imagination, dreaming, and memory through which it clings to the past and future dimensions of time. The mind with these functions and qualities is limited in scope and cannot know the objective truth about anything. The mind is not the true knower: It can calculate, make predictions in time, infer implications, quote authority, make hypotheses, or speculate about the nature of reality, but it cannot see objects directly, from the inside, as they really are in themselves.

In order to allow direct seeing to take place, the mind, which by its very nature attempts to mediate between the object and the subject, has to be quieted. When the mind is totally silent and totally alert, both the real subject *(purusha)* and the real object *(prakriti)* are simultaneously present to it. When the seer is there and what is to be seen is there, seeing takes place without distortion.

Then there is no comparing or judging, no misunderstanding, no fantasizing about things displaced in space and time, no dozing off in heedlessness nor any clinging to past knowledge or experience; in short, there are no distortions introduced by the organs of perception, namely the mind, the feelings, and the senses. There is simply seeing in the present, the living moment in the eternal now. That is the state of perfect and free attention, *kaivalya*, which is the aloneness of seeing, and not of the seer separated from the seen, as it is often misunderstood by commentators on Yoga. In this state, the seer sees through the organs of perception rather than with them.

It is of utmost importance from the point of view of Yoga to distinguish clearly between the mind *(chitta)* and the real Seer *(purusha)*. *Chitta* pretends to know, but it is of the nature of the known and the seen, that is, it is an object rather than a subject. However, it can be an instrument of knowledge.

This misidentification of the seer and the seen, of the person with his organs of perception, is the fundamental error from which all other problems and sufferings arise *(Yoga Sūtras* 2.3–17). It is from this fundamental ignorance that *asmitā* (I-am-this-ness, egoism) arises, creating a limitation by particularization. *Purusha* says, "I AM"; *asmitā* says, "I am this" or "I am that." From this egoism and self-importance comes the strong desire to perpetuate the specialization of oneself and the resulting separation from all else. The sort of "knowledge" that is based on this misidentification is always colored with pride and a tendency to control or to fear.

The means for freedom from the ignorance that is the cause of all sorrow is an unceasing vision of discernment *(viveka khyāti);* such vision alone can permit transcendental insight *(prajñā)* to arise. Nothing can force the appearance of this insight; all one can do is to prepare the ground for it.

The purpose of *prakriti* is to lead to such insight, as that of a seed is to produce fruit; what an aspirant needs to do in preparing the garden is to remove the weeds that choke the full development of the plant. The ground to be prepared is the entire psychosomatic organism, for it is through that organism that *purusha* sees and *prajñā* arises, not through the mind alone, nor the emotions, nor the physical body by itself. A person with dulled senses has as little possibility of coming to *prajñā* as the one with a stupid mind or hardened feelings. Agitation in any part of the entire organism causes fluctuations in attention and muddies the seeing. This is the reason that Yoga puts so much emphasis on the preparation of the body for coming to true knowledge. It is by reversing the usual tendencies of the organism that its agitations can be quieted and the mind can know its right and proper place with respect to *purusha:* that of the *known* rather than the *knower* *(Yoga Sūtras* 2.10, 4.18–20; Ravindra, "Yoga: The Royal Path").

SAMYAMA ATTENTION AS THE INSTRUMENT OF KNOWLEDGE

In classical Yoga, there are eight limbs: the first five are concerned with the purification and preparation of the body, emotions, and breathing and with acquiring the right attitude; the last three limbs are called inner limbs compared with the first five which are relatively outer. The last three are *dhāranā, dhāyna,* and *samādhi. Dhāranā* is concentration in which the consciousness is bound to a single spot. *Dhāyna,* from which the Japanese *Zen* derives through the Chinese *Ch'an* and Korean *Sôn,* is the contemplation or meditative absorption in which there is an uninterrupted flow of attention from the observer to the observed. In these two limbs, the observer acts as the center of consciousness, which sees. When that center is removed, that is to say when the observing is done by *purusha,* through the mind emptied of itself, that state is called *samādhi.* It is a state of silence, settled intelligence, and emptied mind, in which the mind becomes the object to which it attends, and which it reflects truly, as it is.

The insight obtained in the state of *samādhi* is truth-bearing *(ritambhara);* the scope and nature of this knowledge is different from the knowledge gained by the mind or the senses. The insight of *prajñā* reveals the unique particularity, rather than an abstract generality, of an object. Unlike a mental knowledge, in which there is an opposition between the object and the subjective mind, an opposition that inevitably leads to sorrow, the insight of *prajñā,* born of the sustained vision of discernment, is said to be the "deliverer." This insight can be about any object, large or small, far or near, and about any time—past, present, or future—for it is without time-sequence, present everywhere at once, like a photon in physics in its own frame of reference.

The three inner limbs of Yoga, namely, *dhāranā, dhāyna,* and *samādhi,* taken together, constitute what is called *samyama* ("discipline, constraint, gathering"). It is the application of *samyama* to any object that leads to the direct perception of it, because in that state the mind is like a transparent jewel that takes on the true color of the object with which it fuses (*Yoga Sūtras* 1.41). The special attention that prevails in the state of *samyama* can be brought to bear on anything that can be an object of perception, however subtle, that is, on any aspect of *prakriti.*

THE NATURAL SCIENCE OF YOGA

The basic research method of the science of nature according to Yoga is to bring a completely quiet mind and to wait without agitation or projection, letting the object reveal itself in its own true nature, by coloring the transparent mind with its own color. This science is further extended by the principle of analogy and isomorphism between the macrocosmos and the microcosmos, which is the human organism. Therefore, self-knowledge is understood to lead to a knowledge of the cosmos. An example of this isomorphism is to be found in the Yoga Darshana Upanishad (4.48–53), where the external *tīrtha* ("sacred fords, places of pilgrimage, holy waters") are identified with the various parts of the organism: "The Mount Meru is in the head and Kedara in your brow; between your eyebrows, near your nose, know dear disciple, that Varanasi stands; in your heart is the confluence of the Ganga and the Yamuna."

A large number of aphorisms in the *Yoga Sūtras* (3.16 –53) describe the knowledge and the powers gained by attending to various objects in the state of *samyama*. For example, we are told that, through *samyama* on the sun, one gains insight into the solar system, and by *samyama* on the moon, knowledge of the arrangement of the stars (*Yoga Sūtras* 3.26–27). Similarly, many occult and extraordinary powers *(siddhis)* accrue to the Yogi by bringing the state of *samyama* to bear upon various aspects of oneself: For example, by *samyama* on the relation between the ear and space, one acquires the divine ear by which one can hear at a distance or hear extremely subtle and usually inaudible sounds. Many other powers are mentioned by Patañjali; however, they are not his main concern. He does not suggest that there is anything wrong with these powers; no more does he suggest that there is anything wrong with the mind. The point is rather that the mind in itself is an inadequate instrument for gaining true knowledge; similarly, these powers, however vast and fascinating, are inadequate as the goal of true knowledge.

It is wrong to suggest that Yoga is not interested in the knowledge of nature and is occupied only with self-knowledge. From the perspective of Yoga, this is an erroneous distinction to start with, simply because any self that can be known, however subtle, is a part of nature and is not separate from it. The deepest self, to which alone belong true seeing and knowing, cannot be known; but it can be identified with. One can become that self *(Atman, Purusha)* and know with it, from its level, with its clarity. In no way is *prakriti* considered unreal or merely a mental projection; it is very real, and though it can overwhelm the mind with its dynamism and charms and veil the truth, yet in its proper place and function it exists in order to serve the real person *(purusha)*.

It is, however, certainly true that the procedures, methods, attitudes, and perceptions involved in Yoga are radically different from those in modern science, as are the aims of the two types of knowledge (cf. chapter 3, "Perception in Yoga and Physics," in this volume). Briefly, one can say that, in contradistinction to modern science, the knowledge in Yoga is a third-eye knowledge, transformational in character. It is a knowledge that does not do violence to the object of its investigation; it is a knowledge by participation, rather than by standing apart or against the object. Knowledge in Yoga is primarily for the sake of true seeing and the corresponding freedom (Ravindra, *Whispers*, esp. chs. 1, 2, and 6).

Yoga and Prana

Proper breathing plays an extremely important function in Yoga. The quality of breathing in a person is intimately and directly related with the person's inner state, as is apparent from even a superficial observation of oneself. The traditional appreciation of this fact is reflected in all ancient, particularly scriptural, languages, in which the words for "spirit," "breath," and "air" are either the same or very close to each other. This is true, for example, in Sanskrit, Pali, Chinese, Hebrew, Arabic, and Greek.

One of the eight limbs of classical Yoga is *Prānāyāma*, which involves training in right breathing. *Prāna*, which is translated as "breath," is in fact the whole subtle energy of life, connecting mind with consciousness. *Prāna* is said to be present everywhere at all times. In Indian thought, *prāna* is equated with *Purusha, Atman,* the cosmic essence, and *Brahman*. It is the vital energy that animates every being. The quality of one's being corresponds to the quality of *prāna*. The similar concept of *chi, qi,* or *ki* in the Chinese, Korean, and Japanese traditions is very close to that of *prāna* in Indian thought, with a similar range of breadth and subtlety, as well as similar difficulty of explication in the usual scientific terms.

Even at the most ordinary level of physical culture, tremendous feats of strength are accomplished by people who are able to control their breath. However, it is important to emphasize that the *prāna* that is subtler and closer to the spirit *(purusha, pneuma)* cannot be manipulated or controlled from below, by the mind or the body. What one can do is to allow the mind and the body to be pervaded by the subtle *prāna*, which by itself will bring about an alchemical transformation of the organism, making it more and more sensitive.

Thus, in the final analysis, it is less a matter of controlling *prāna* and more a matter of being controlled by *prāna*. Therein lies the chief difficulty in making a scientific study of *prāna:* What can be studied by the mind in the modern scientific mode is only what can in some senses be manipulated and controlled by the mind and is thus below the level of the mind (cf. chapter 7, "Experience and Experiment," in this volume). In the presence of something higher than itself, the mind needs to learn how to be quiet and to listen.

Another remark needs to be made about the various practices of Yoga: What is below cannot coerce what is above. One cannot force higher consciousness or spirit by any manipulation of the body or the breath. A right physical posture or moral conduct may aid internal development, but it does not determine it or guarantee it. More often external behavior reflects internal development. For example, a person does not necessarily become wise by breathing or thinking in a particular way; but a person breathes and thinks in that way because he or she is wise. Actions reflect being more than they affect it.

CHAPTER SIX

SCIENCE AND THE SACRED

Science, and indeed all intellectual work, has a sacred nature that must be recovered, asserted, and celebrated. When the intellect is not oriented toward and serving Divine Wisdom, it is bound to become a force for fragmentation, self-serving, and evil.

For some of the greatest scientists, science has been a spiritual path, a way to connect with and serve the Sacred. Rightly understood and oriented, it can be so again. The best scientists have always approached science as a sacred activity—an activity that can yield "the secrets of the Old One," as Einstein put it (cf. chapter 10, "Science as a Spiritual Path," in this volume). In his own words, Kepler was—and by extension every scientist potentially is—"a priest of God in the temple of Nature" (Ravindra, "Kepler").

Einstein (*Essays* 112–3) stated the sacred nature of science:

> It is, of course, universally agreed, that science has to establish connections between the facts of experience, of such a kind that we can predict further occurrences from those already experienced. Indeed, according to the opinion of many positivists the completest possible accomplishment of this task is the only end of science. I do not believe, however, that so elementary an ideal could do much to kindle the investigator's passion from which really great achievements have arisen. Behind the tireless efforts of an investigator there lurks a stronger, more mysterious drive: it is existence and reality that one wishes to comprehend.

On another occasion, referring to the very high quality scientific work of Max Planck, Einstein (*Essays* 5) said, "The state of mind that enables a man to do work of this kind is akin to that of the religious worshipper or the lover." And again (*Essays* 11), "Certain it is that a conviction, akin to religious feeling, of the rationality or the intelligibility of the world lies behind all scientific work of a higher order."

THE SACRED

Einstein did not use the phrase "religious feeling" in any sectarian or churchly sense; he meant a feeling of awe, mystery, subtlety, and vastness—precisely the feeling one has in the presence of the Sacred. In another context (*Ideas and Opinions* 39) he called it a "cosmic religious feeling" that he regarded as the "strongest and noblest motive for scientific research." This feeling is

> one of rapturous amazement at the harmony of natural law, which reveals an intelligence of such superiority that, compared with it, all the systematic thinking and acting of human beings is an utterly insignificant reflection. . . . The most beautiful thing we can experience is the mysterious. It is the source of all true art and science. . . . To know that what is impenetrable to us really exists, manifesting itself as the highest wisdom and the most radiant beauty which our dull faculties can comprehend only in their most primitive forms—this knowledge, this feeling, is at the center of true religiousness. In this sense, and in this sense only, I belong in the ranks of devoutly religious men. (Einstein, *Ideas and Opinions* 11)

What Einstein here refers to as "true religiousness" is a subtle combination of feeling and knowledge, a total human response to the Sacred, which is immeasurably higher than any human faculty can comprehend but which touches human beings as it touches everything else in the cosmos (Ravindra, "Einstein"). It is this that human beings—at their best—have always wished to know, have always loved, and have always tried to serve. Labels and designations have naturally varied from culture to culture and from century to century, but it—the superpersonal Wisdom, Intelligence, Being, God, Mystery, Vastness, Truth, Love, Tao, One, or That—is the Sacred. It is what enlightens the Buddha, anoints the Christ, motivates Socrates in his love of Wisdom, and makes Krishna draw human beings to himself as the embodiment of the Highest. And it is what enthralls Einstein in his search for cosmological order.

Obstacles to Recognizing the Sacred

How is it, then, that many people these days—some of them thoughtful and of good will—view science as a force opposed to spirituality and as chiefly responsible for the impoverishment and desacralization of nature? The highest motivation of great scientists of the past was to understand the Divine Wisdom through a study of nature and to serve humanity through the technological applications of science. Today, many people seem to associate science with the control and exploitation of nature in the service of a military-industrial complex, underpinned by fear and greed.

What is the reality? Have the motivations of scientists in fact changed? Or have historical and social pressures on scientists forced them to serve ends that may not be in accord with their highest aspirations? Are some of these changes parallel to the differences between the aspirations of the great saints of the past and the concerns of the established churches of today?

Since the end of the eighteenth century, most scientists—the vast majority of whom have been of European extraction with a cultural background of biblical religions—do not describe their relationship with the Sacred in conventional religious terms, especially in terms of faith in a personal God. They feel an incompatibility between science and such a faith. The relationship of scientists with the Sacred is more likely to be expressed these days in terms of wonder, beauty, mathematical harmony, or search for truth, cosmological order, and the unity of laws and forces. Those are all feelings highly valued in the great traditions of the world as marks of a truly spiritual or religious mind.

Perhaps it is the confining of the Divine intelligence to a particular and exclusivist theological formulation in terms of a personal God that makes scientists shy of admitting a sense of the Sacred. To quote Einstein (*Out of My Later Years* 27–9) again:

> The main source of the present-day conflicts between the spheres of religion and of science lies in this concept of a personal God. . . . In their struggle for the ethical good, teachers of religion must have the stature to give up the doctrine of a personal God, that is, give up the source of fear and hope which in the past placed such a vast

power in the hands of priests. In their labors they will have to avail themselves of those forces which are capable of cultivating the Good, the True and the Beautiful in humanity itself. This is, to be sure, a more difficult but an incomparably more worthy task.

As Western religions during the past three centuries have more and more emphasized faith as against reason, scientists have been pushed in the apparently opposite camp of knowledge, experience, and insight (Ravindra, "Physics and Religion"). Also, in the face of the long drawn-out warfare in Europe among the various sects of the Christian faith, many people, including some very spiritually oriented scientists, wished to separate their activities from sectarian religion altogether. But a separation from sectarian religion is not the same as a separation from the Sacred.

Science has become institutionalized on a large scale, especially during the twentieth century, when the contribution of basic science and technology to war efforts was more and more appreciated. As a result, science and technology were deeply intertwined in the minds of both policy makers and the general public. The very close connection of science with technology and the emphasis on the utilitarian aspects of knowledge are bound to have had a deleterious effect on the purer aspirations of scientists, especially when mastery over nature is sundered from the spiritual impulse of transforming our inner nature to serve the Divine.

When we can control much of nature without submitting ourselves to spiritual disciplines that militate against ambition, greed, and hubris, the result is inevitable. Our impulse to exploit nature, other cultures, and other species is unchecked by our higher but uncultivated impulses of compassion and love. It is easy to forget what Einstein (*Ideas and Opinions* 12) said, echoing the insight of all the great spiritual sages of the world: "The true value of a human being is determined primarily by the measure and the sense in which he has attained liberation from the self."

Modern science and technology are the most developed expressions of Western rationality and constitute the major forces of modernity, not only in the West but throughout the world. Everything that is good and desirable about our modern age, as well as everything that is bad and troublesome, has something to do with science and technology, directly or indirectly. Science and technology underline the specificity of contemporary life. Everywhere, people wish to cultivate and use science and technology, which are the *sine qua non* of development. Every nation seems convinced that, without scientific and technological expertise, it would lose its competitive edge, leading to a slide in its standard of living.

On the other hand, a great many thoughtful people everywhere, including those in hyperindustrialized Western societies, are uneasy and feel a sense of helplessness in the face of the accelerating march of technology. The role that was performed by "fate" in primitive societies is now played by the juggernaut of technology in industrially advanced countries. From unbridled technology arises a sense of threat to the environment, to our physical, emotional, and mental well-being, to family and social values, to spirituality, to a sense of relatedness with the cosmos, and to other modes of knowing. Because of its perceived intimate connection with technology, science itself is sometimes viewed as the source of this threat.

The very success of science during the past four centuries in understanding the mysteries of the universe—augmented by its relationship with power structures through technology—has led some scientists to a state of hubris. Whereas great scientists have seldom held that the scientific approach to nature is the only way to understand the whole of reality, some scientists and philosophers of science have concluded that "non-science is non-sense." Not only does such an attitude serve badly the open-ended nature of scientific inquiry, it also imposes on nature a particular and limited view.

At any stage of scientific development, certain assumptions about nature are necessary in order to make observations manageable and communicable to others. But that does not mean that externally measurable and quantifiable aspects of nature are all there is to nature or the rest of reality. As Einstein said, "The most beautiful thing we can experience is the mysterious." To insist on one particular view of nature, as is often done in the name of science, is to impoverish nature as well as humanity.

The history of science shows that science is not a finished or dead activity that cannot undergo radical changes in its assumptions and procedures. Future science, to the extent it radically departs from present-day science, will naturally have different assumptions and procedures. Those who have concluded that science has brought about disenchantment and the death of nature need to remember that science has been a wonderful path to the mysteries of nature, and it is likely to keep bringing people to the gates of Mystery.

Any sensible world order is unimaginable without the contributions of science and technology, which come bearing the promise of prosperity and health. At the same time, some people sense an erosion of values and meaning in human life, which they associate with the rapid industrialization brought about by developments in science and technology. Both the promise and the threat of science and technology are felt by thoughtful and sensitive people everywhere, but even more strongly in non-Western traditional societies.

Will traditional modes of knowing—some of which have long histories and outstanding practical applications, especially in physical and emotional healing and family and social relationships—be marginalized by modern science and technology? Are non-Western cultures required to accept Western philosophical, religious, and social ideas when they adopt science and technology? Military and industrial power depends on science and technology, and no one wishes to be without power. But some leaders of traditional cultures believe that Western societies have won such power at the cost of spiritual and human values, acquiring power without wisdom and compassion.

A recovery of the spiritual values inherent in the practice of science would help to heal our modern world, in which science plays such a crucial and vital role, for both the West and the East. This recovery would certainly be harmonious with the ideals and aspirations of the great scientists.

SCIENCE IN THE INSIGHT TRADITIONS AND IN THE FAITH TRADITIONS

Scientific knowledge has a very different function and place in the West and in the East. Western culture has been spiritually nurtured by faith-oriented biblical traditions, especially Christianity, whereas Eastern cultures have been nourished by the insight-oriented traditions of Hinduism and Buddhism. An example will illustrate their difference.

Albert Einstein (*Ideas and Opinions* 46) once remarked, "Science without religion is lame, religion without science is blind." That sounds congenial and heartwarming, especially for those whose religious feelings are assaulted in the name of science. But let us explore this remark a little further.

There is a parallel remark by Ishvarakrishna in the *Sānkhyakārikā* from the second century B.C.E. This is a very important text in the Indian tradition because it deals with the theory of Sānkhya, which is very closely allied with its practical counterpart, namely, Yoga. Yoga in its turn is at the very heart of Indian spirituality. The *Sānkhyakārikā* almost certainly influenced the much better known *Yoga Sūtras* of Patañjali, a very slim volume that has had an incalculable influence on the spiritual life of India. Talking about *purusha* and *prakriti*, which we may translate as "spirit" and "nature," Ishvarakrishna says, "Purusha without prakriti is lame, prakriti without purusha is blind."

These two statements are so alike that a professor seeing them on two student papers would naturally suspect plagiarism! But the two statements are so widely separated in time, space, and culture and so clearly from independent and seminal minds that we should simply celebrate the happy similarity. If we look at the two statements closely, however, we discover a world of difference.

Whatever else we understand by the metaphors of "blind" and "lame," we certainly associate insight, clarity, light, and illumination with the opposite of blindness, namely sight. All the great teachers say in one way or another that we have eyes but do not see, and that we have ears but do not hear. To see clearly is a mark of wisdom. Being lame, on the other hand, implies inability to act, lack of will, incapacity, and lack of movement or involvement.

Therefore Einstein says that vision—insight, wisdom, clarity, illumination—comes from science, but mobility—motivation, action, will, and emotion—come from religion. For Ishvarakrishna, on the other hand, insight—*jñāna* (knowledge), *prajñā* (wisdom), *bodhi* (enlightenment)—belong to *purusha*. Action, movement, and emotion—the realm of the *gunas* or constituents of nature—belong to *prakriti*.

Now, we have a very interesting situation emerging: We would all agree, including Einstein, if he were here and willing to engage with us using the same language, that science has to do with *prakriti* which literally means "nature," because that is what the natural sciences try to study. Also the word *physis* in Greek, from which we get the word "physics," means "nature." Religion, on the other hand, as Einstein might agree with the popular opinion, deals with what is beyond nature, thus with what is supernatural. If we appreciate the delicacy of the situation, we see some very interesting differences in what the East and the West understand by "science" and "religion."

For the scientific West, knowledge and reasoning pertain to the domain of nature, but the spiritual realm is completely discontinuous with nature—it is supernatural in that sense—and is a matter of faith. By extension from knowledge, wisdom and insight also tend to have their source in the study of nature, namely in science. In the East, on the other hand, insight and wisdom are understood to result from clearer consciousness of higher spiritual realms, and scientific study of nature can provide the means for carrying out the actions resulting from insight.

In the East, the basic diagnosis of the human situation is that our whole predicament arises from ignorance *(avidyā)*. The root cause of all our difficulties is ignorance. From that arises the confusion between the Self and the non-Self (Vedanta), or between *nitya* (eternal) and *anitya* (transient) and a clinging to the world of *anitya*. Thus arise fear and fantasy, *dukkha* (suffering), *māyā* (illusion), and *asmitā* (egoism). For the Buddha, Shankara, Patañjali, and all other great teachers of India, the root of all our problems is ignorance. If we know rightly, right action will naturally follow. If insight leads to and controls action and guides it, then there is right order, both internally and externally. In other words, when *purusha*—consciousness, spirit, seeing (which is the sole function of *Purusha*, the Seer, according to Patañjali's *Yoga Sūtras* 2.20)—sees and leads *Prakriti*, there is awakening, enlightenment, freedom, moksha, and nirvana. Otherwise, a person is bound in *dukkha, māyā, asmitā,* and the *kleshas* (obstacles)!

In the Western biblical religions, the situation is quite different. The basic human problem is not ignorance; it is rather self-will. In general, from the biblical point of view, to say that we are waiting to engage in right action until we know rightly is just excuse-making. God has revealed what needs to be known; we know what the right action is. Our problem is that we do not want to obey the commandments and get on with the right action. We want to follow and act according to our own self-will, rather than God's will. "Nothing burneth in hell except self-will," says the *Theologia Germanica* (ch. 34). And the whole exquisite agony of the cross—the way of the Christ (Ravindra, *Christ the Yogi* 151–2)—is in his last words in the Garden of Gethsemane: "If it is possible, let this cup pass me by. Yet, not my will, but thine be done" (Mark 14.36).

In the East, the need is for true knowledge, because right knowledge leads to right action. In the West, the need is for true action in obedience to the will of God, because right action leads to right knowledge. In the West, one is likely to be told, "Don't just sit there, do something." In the East, the wise are likely to advise, "Don't just do something, sit there."

Bodhidharma is one of the major patriarchs of Zen Buddhism. He is the last Indian patriarch in the line from the Buddha through his great disciple Mahakashyapa; then the line of the patriarchs moves to China, and later to Japan. When Bodhidharma first went to China to teach the dharma, what did he do on arriving there? Did he study the sociopolitical situation? Did he meet the leaders? Did he arrange religious evangelical crusades, or organize a poster campaign, or have social elites sit with him on the podium impressing the folk? No, he went and sat in a cave, facing a wall! We might think he would soon get up. Maybe after a few hours or days or months. No. He sat for twelve years alone in a cave, facing a wall. Then he understood the way it is, what needed to be done, and he got up and started doing it: teaching Tai Chi to prepare the Chinese bodies for meditation, undertaking massive translation projects, but above all teaching how to do nothing and just to sit. "Sitting" is *za* in Japanese and "meditation" is *zen* (from Sanskrit *dhyāna*), hence *zazen* is "sitting meditation." According to Dogen Zenzi of the twelfth century, "Zen is nothing but zazen."

The heart of meditation is to do nothing, just to sit, with stillness and silence of the body, mind, and emotions, so quietly that one can hear a rose petal fall, the sound of thoughts arising, and the silence between thoughts. The arising of thoughts and emotions is part of the play of *prakriti*, and watching this play with complete equanimity, without being disturbed, belongs to *purusha*. Without the presence of the seeing *purusha*, *prakriti* is blind, lost in agitated movement and action; but *purusha* needs *prakriti* for purposive activity. Thus, a sage does nothing, but everything is accomplished. Lao-tzu said, "The Tao of the sage is to work without effort." Krishnamurti said, "Be totally attentive and do nothing."

Given this fundamental difference between the East and the West in their understanding of what religion is about, it is not surprising that Einstein should place religion on the side of action, movement, and motivation. Insight, practically by default, falls on the side of science, a study of the dance of *prakriti* and a part of *prakriti*. Because science deals with the measurement of space, time, and materiality, it cannot be *purusha*. As noted in chapter 4, the great physicist Max Planck said, "That which cannot be measured is not real." Spirit, by definition, is not restricted to measurement, space, time, or materiality. The word *māyā* or "illusion," on the other hand, is derived from the same root as "meter" and "measurement." So the sages of India could easily have said, "What can be measured cannot possibly be Real."

RECONCILIATION OF THE PARADOX

Thus we have an interesting paradox with respect to two very similar sounding statements from two very great minds. How do we reconcile them? An ordinary contradiction may be a sign that one side is right and the other wrong. But a profound paradox is not a contradiction that requires us to choose one side or the other. Such paradoxes often remind us about the limitations of language, logic, and thought when they concern really important things. Niels Bohr used to say that the opposite of a great truth is another great truth.

Every great teacher has recognized that what is really True and Real cannot be expressed in words or grasped by the rational mind. What can be said is not worth saying in some ultimate sense. And what is really worth saying cannot be said. On the other hand, science is the only activity in our modern world, especially in the West, that is oriented to truth, reason, and knowledge. Because these are the characteristics associated with insight or vision, it is not surprising that many intelligent and sensitive young people in the West, who have a scientific mode in their education but who still have a sense of the Sacred, are naturally drawn to the spiritual traditions of the East. However, the nature of insight, knowledge, and perceptions in the domain of science is quite different from that in the realm of spirituality—as different as the realms of *prakriti* and *purusha* (cf. chapter 3, "Perception in Yoga and Physics," in this volume).

How might we recast the statement of Einstein or Ishvarakrishna? We might say, for example, "Insight without compassionate action is lame, and compassion without wisdom is blind." All sages have said that true insight naturally flowers into compassion and love, like the fragrance of a rose. A Buddha who is awake but is without compassion is an oxymoron. But we can certainly have a stupid saint, just as we can have an ineffective scholar or a philosophy professor who cannot change a light bulb!

Any true reconciliation of science and spirituality is not to be found in a coexistence of abstractions. Spiritual, unlike scientific, truth is always a matter of direct perception. Patañjali (*Yoga Sūtras* 1.49) said, "The knowledge based on inference and testimony is different from direct knowledge [obtained in higher states of consciousness] because it pertains to a particular object." This is why biblical traditions have tenaciously held to the experience of God who is a unique Person, or *Purusha Vishesha,* in the *Yoga Sūtras* (1.24).

In still higher states of consciousness, perception may shift from minute particulars embedded in wholeness to undifferentiated Oneness so that what remains is Pure Seeing without anything seen apart from it. Yet spiritual vision always remains a matter of direct perception. Whatever difficulties Einstein may have had with the notion of a personal God, religious perception is not of the same kind as a philosophic or scientific generalization and abstraction. Pascal was truer to the biblical understanding of God because he always kept on his person the declaration "God of Abraham, Isaac, and Jacob—not of the philosophers and scholars." For him God was a matter of experience, not an inference from a philosophical proposition or a scientific hypothesis.

Two forms of awareness can reside in the same person: on the one hand, direct religious supersensuous perceptions and, on the other, reasoned scientific theorizing and experimentation with its corresponding philosophical abstractions—however rare actual instances of this may be. The reconciliation of religion and science needs to take place in the soul of the same whole person so that there can be purposive action without self-centeredness, individuality without egoism, wholeness without loss of uniqueness. In fact, this very reconciliation took place within Einstein himself, in spite of his occasional lapses into polemic theologizing behind the shield of science. For him, as for many great scientists, the Sacred was not discovered or proved by science. The Sacred called them, pervaded their lives, and gave significance to their scientific activity, as it would have to their other activities, such as music or poetry or painting, if they had been called to celebrate the Sacred through the arts, as were Bach, Kalidasa, and El Greco.

Perhaps we could recast the paradoxical statements as "Religion without scientific knowledge is ineffective, but science without religious perception is insignificant."

EXPERIENCE AND EXPERIMENT: A CRITIQUE OF MODERN SCIENTIFIC KNOWING

Nowadays, all intellectual activities are supposed to be scientific. "Scientific" is almost synonymous with reasonable, rigorous, systematic, and desirable. The classical ideal of seeking the true, the beautiful, and the good is replaced, at least in universities, by an effort to be scientific. The force of the mystique and metaphysics of science becomes particularly apparent in philosophical, psychological, and religious studies, where the scientific stick has been widely used to drive out a great deal of sensitive feeling and imaginative thought.

If we use the etymological meaning of the word "science" (from Latin *scientia*, "knowledge"), we might wonder how anyone could question the obvious desirability of knowledge. But to do this would be to rely on ancient meanings that are related to the present intellectual climate by very thin threads indeed. Presumably, when people talk about the scientific study of something, they have a model of the natural sciences in mind. It is obvious that these sciences operate from many fundamental assumptions about the nature of human beings, truth, and reality; most of these metaphysical presuppositions have been incorporated into the contemporary social sciences and the humanities to their detriment. Here I point out some of these assumptions and discuss their validity and limitations (as also, from a somewhat different perspective, in chapter 4, "Western Science and Technology and the Indian Intellectual Tradition," in this volume). What is proposed is a radical reexamination and reevaluation of scientific knowledge.

The study of human beings is not fundamentally different from the study of nature, nor should it be based on different principles. On the contrary, the sundering of human beings and nature is built right into the presuppositions of the modern sciences and is entirely questionable. If scientific studies have not yielded any understanding of what it means to be a person, that lack does not imply the disunity of person and nature, and consequently of knowledge about them. Perhaps the methods of the natural sciences are no more beyond question in studying nature than they are in studying human beings. It may only be that with human beings, some of the metaphysical restrictions and limitations of science become more apparent.

Those who attempt to understand human beings seem willing either to leave nature to the scientists, as if people had nothing to do with nature, or to utilize scientific procedures that inevitably lead to the impoverishment of human beings, as they do also of nature. If for us science-nurtured moderns, cosmology has become a branch of physics, then it should come as no surprise that a human being is merely an aggregate of material particles.

The tragedy of post-Renaissance intellectual life is that very few thinkers have included nature, human beings, and divinity in a unified continuum of investigation based, not only on speculative concepts, but also on experience and perceptions. Perhaps the only well-known exception is Goethe. His criticism of Newtonian science, unlike that of Blake or Wordsworth, has the merit of being reasoned and consistent, as well as having a detailed theory for doing science with alternative and more unifying assumptions. However, his influence in scientific circles has been negligible. Newton's own theology and alchemy are fascinating but show little continuity with his science. This lack of a unified approach to the world is the result of an inner fragmentation in which person and nature are separated from each other, as are poetry and physics. The fragmentation is embodied in the very structure of the modern sciences.

The central core of any theory of knowledge, including science, involves a triad of the knower, reality, and the connection between them. Different theories and practices emphasize different aspects of human beings (reason, feeling, sensation) or of reality (quantity, quality, mechanism, purpose) or of the connection between these two (repeatability, uniqueness, intersubjectivity, involvement). No great theory wholly ignores any one of these several aspects.

The differences between theories are largely in their emphasis and underlying faith about what is primary and irreducible, by which everything else must be explained. The scientific faith holds that quantity is basic and that all qualities must be explained in quantitative terms. When a theory of knowledge satisfies and is successful, according to our valuation of its purpose and accomplishments, it can easily become established as "the" way to truth, making doubters into heretics.

Perhaps the most important innovation of the great scientific revolution of the sixteenth and seventeenth centuries was a restructuring of the triad of knowledge, with an insistence that empirical observations lead to truth, which cannot be approached by reasoning alone. Having been conditioned by centuries of scientific success, our very notion of rationality is now based on this model of scientific procedure. It is now difficult for us to realize that whatever the scientific revolution was about, it was not universally considered a triumph of reason. Whitehead (*Science and the Modern World*, ch. 1) has correctly observed, "Science has never shaken off the impress of its origin in the historical revolt of the late Renaissance. It has remained predominantly an anti-rationalist movement, based on a naive faith."

Modern science was clearly a necessary reaction to the rationalistic extravagance of the scholastics. However, perhaps like all revolutions, the scientific revolution was based on simplistic assumptions. It swept away much in earlier thought that was useful and wise and in harmony with reality. Also by accepting a limited criterion of truth, it guaranteed an inner fragmentation of human beings. In spite of later considerable upheavals within scientific theories, the basic attitudes and presuppositions of the modern sciences remain essentially the same as those that emerged during the revolution. From these we derive most of our scientific outlook, even in the humanities.

On a large historical scale, the relatively recent appearance of the scientific attitude should itself be a reminder that humanity can exist without it. Many signs, widespread at present, particularly among the young, suggest that unless the metaphysical basis of science is broadened to include much that has been arbitrarily excluded, we shall soon be ushered into a postscientific age. Any enlargement of the scientific base is likely to come about mainly within the scientific community. We cannot exclude the possibility of some useful contribution from outside, but in general most nonscientists are awed and overwhelmed by science into wishful acquiescence or frightened hostility. Science needs neither worship nor rejection, but critical self-understanding and change. This need has always existed; now it has become urgent. To the extent that science is an avenue to Truth—with a capital T, which most scientists tacitly believe, however unsophisticated it may appear in the modern age—scientists must be interested in the kind of knowledge they produce. A master scientist, Albert Einstein, said:

> How does a normally talented research scientist come to concern himself with the theory of knowledge? Is there not more valuable work to be done in his field? I hear this from many of my professional colleagues; or rather, I sense in the case of many more of them that this is what they feel.
>
> I cannot share this opinion. When I think of the ablest students whom I have encountered in teaching—i.e., those who distinguish themselves by their independence of judgment, and not only by mere agility—I find that they had a lively concern for the theory of knowledge. They liked to start discussions concerning the aims and methods of the sciences, and showed unequivocally by the obstinacy with which they defended their views that this subject seemed important to them.
>
> This is really not astonishing. For when I turn to science not for some superficial reason such as money-making or ambition, and also not (or at least exclusively) for the pleasure of the sport, the delights of brain-athletics, then the following questions must burningly interest me as a disciple of this science: What goal will and can be reached by the science to which I am dedicating myself? To what extent are its general results "true"? What is essential, and what is based only on the accidents of development?
>
> Concepts which have proved useful for ordering things easily assume so great an authority over us, that we forget their terrestrial origin and accept them as unalterable facts. They then become labeled as "conceptual necessities," "a priori situations," etc. The road of scientific progress is frequently blocked for long periods by such errors. It is therefore not just an idle game to exercise our ability to analyze familiar concepts, and to demonstrate the conditions on

which their justification and usefulness depend, and the way in which these developed, little by little. (quoted by Holton, *Thematic Origins of Scientific Thought* 5)

EXPERIMENT AND EXPERIENCE

One of the most important reasons for the avowed success of the natural sciences in investigating nature has been a particular wedding of a restricted notion of a human being, essentially as a rational cognizer, and a limited class of experience, namely experiment. It was the coming together of these two, reason and experiment, in a mutually regenerative role that characterized the scientific revolution and all subsequent science.

In the formation of the scientific attitude to nature, experiments play a large role, for they are what ultimately constitute the scientist's handle on reality. An experiment is anything connecting scientific perceptions and conceptions; in other words, all the means and procedures for collecting scientific data, including observations, tests, and surveys. The central place of experiment in the sciences is beyond question. No scientist will question the statement of Richard Feynman on the first page of a highly successful physics textbook *(Feynmann Lectures on Physics):* "The principle of science, the definition, almost, is the following: The test of all knowledge is experiment. Experiment is the sole judge of scientific 'truth.' "

It is important to distinguish between *experiment* and *experience*, although these two terms are often used interchangeably in scientific and philosophical writings. There are significant differences in their connotations and applications. The sciences by no means have a monopoly on observational and empirical procedures; aesthetics and spirituality are nothing if not empirical. In the sciences, however, it is ultimately the external experiment that is the arbiter of the truth of one theory against another.

In the sphere of spiritual becoming, on the other hand, the central focus is the inner experience of the aspirant. Without corresponding experimental data, scientific speculation tends to become sterile and fruitless; similarly, without reference to experience, all theological talk remains empty, full of comfort and hope perhaps, but not charged with real understanding. To make bedfellows of Francis Bacon and St. Paul, one could say that neither scientific knowledge nor spiritual understanding is a matter of talk; in either case it is a matter of power. The nature of this power depends on where the criteria of truth and falsity are centered—in experiment or experience. Both mediate between human beings and reality but differently, and with quite divergent consequences.

The words "experience" (from Latin *experientia*) and "experiment" (from Latin *experimentum*) are both derived ultimately from the Latin verb *experiri*, meaning "to try thoroughly." The root of that verb, *periri*, is also related to the English words "peril" and "fare," meaning "travel," as in "wayfarer." To experience something or experiment with it is to try it out thoroughly, involving some personal risk; it is to be there, to travel through it. The knowledge obtained by such a procedure is what we call understanding or comprehension. Experience, especially, includes perceptions, feelings, and sensings. The word "experiment," on the other hand, during the last three hundred years has diverged in meaning. To experiment now is primarily to conduct an experiment, a test made to demonstrate a known truth, to examine the validity of a hypothesis, or to determine the efficacy of something previously untried. The knowledge obtained by these procedures is what constitutes scientific knowledge. Clearly, experimental sciences are not experiential in character.

Galileo seems to have been the first modern scientist clearly to differentiate between these two concepts; before him *experientia* and *experimentum* were more or less indiscriminately used. He says in his "De motu": "Those things which we have demonstrated . . . must be understood as referring to moving bodies which are free from all external resistance, but since it is perhaps impossible to find such bodies in the material world, anyone performing an experiment concerning these things should not be surprised if the (resulting) experience disappoints, and that a large sphere cannot be moved by a minimal force, even if in a horizontal plane" (*Opere* 1:300 –1).

For Galileo, experience is presumably what one actually sees, and experiment is the procedure of testing a hypothesis. His hypothesis pertains to a conjectured ideal and rational world in which one can imagine ideal bodies free from all external resistance. Because of their ideal and rational nature, they can be reasoned about mathematically; inferences from this reasoning process are what he subjects to experimental test. Whatever the nature of this abstract theoretical construction may be, the testing procedure does not depend on experience in the sense of personal, existential, involvement.

Galileo's *Dialogue Concerning the Two Chief World Systems* makes it clear that the experimental method of knowledge is empirical only in a special and limited sense and that it is certainly not experiential. What we apprehend directly with our mind, feelings, and senses is not what we depend on for true scientific knowledge. Feelings and senses are particularly suspect. Galileo commended Copernicus and his followers who "have through sheer force of intellect done such violence to their own senses as to prefer what reason told them over that which sensible experience plainly showed them to the contrary."

On this attitude toward feelings and the senses depends the all-important distinction between primary and secondary qualities, which was crucial to the development of physics and the scientific notion of objectivity. Exclusion of the immediacy of perceptions and feelings is central to the scientific procedure; what one does in scientific experiments is to measure, not experience, but certain qualities of things. This measuring can be done indirectly without the scientists seeing or feeling what they are measuring, and indeed without their being involved at all in the actual event of observing and recording, which can be done automatically. Successful experimenters can arrange matters so that they do not have to be present in the laboratory when data are collected about the scattering of electrons or the overcrowding of rats or the contraction of the uterus in childbirth.

The "personal equation" is something a scientist must assiduously attempt to eliminate. The scientist is indeed needed to interpret and manipulate data, imagine new hypotheses, and devise new experiments. Obviously, none of these activities is easy or trivial; they call for a great deal of cleverness, ingenuity, and sometimes genius. Nevertheless, for the observations themselves, which provide the only direct scientific contact with reality, no human intervention is strictly speaking necessary, certainly not of the feelings and most of the senses.

What kind of data can be gathered by ignoring so much of what makes us human? What reality is revealed by observations that can be made by properly programmed automatons? What sort of theories can be tested or satisfied with such impoverished data? What significance can be claimed for knowledge based on such determinedly partial perceptions? These questions call for detailed and careful investigation, particularly today, when most academics have raised the scientific method to an intellectual orthodoxy.

Perhaps we have been dazzled by the magical successes of science and technology into accepting unwarranted metaphysical assumptions about the nature of reality and of human beings and their relationship with each other. These assumptions are partial, and they necessarily lead to a further fragmentation of our sensibilities, resulting in an attitude of inner violence toward the object of investigation. The procedures based on them are quite unlikely to lead to a sympathetic understanding of either nature or human beings. In particular, the divided self that is an inevitable consequence of the scientific mentality cannot even approach what is higher, within us or above us.

Clearly, many metaphysical assumptions underlie the scientific enterprise. Most of these assumptions are now widely taken to be valid in the humanities also, indicating the wholesale capitulation of the intellectual community and the pervasive influence of science. This influence asserts itself through something labeled "the scientific method," which many of the nonscientific academic disciplines are especially anxious to get hold of.

It is difficult to find examples in intellectual history in which creative thinking proceeded from methodology to practice. Even Descartes, who made so much of method, wrote his *Discourse on Method* after the scientific essays to which it forms a preface, and not before. It is only in the contemporary social sciences that one finds so much faith in the efficacy of verbalized methodology. Among the natural sciences, few departments offer their students a course on method. The method is simply, as I think P. W. Bridgman said, to do one's damnedest best with no holds barred. Nevertheless, there are basic assumptions underlying the scientific procedures; these assumptions are handed down by tradition and are in general acquired by students unconsciously.

OBJECTIVITY

The locus of scientific objectivity is not in the object under investigation, but in the subjects investigating the object. What we call objectivity in the sciences is intersubjectivity; we say that we have come to an objective description of something if most of the competent investigators—that is, those who share the same assumptions and procedures—agree with each other about this description. Whether the description actually describes the object is another matter; we do not even know how we might determine this unless we were to allow the possibility that the object knows itself and reveals itself. But such a concession of consciousness and intention to any object runs directly counter to the basic scientific conception of the cosmos as a huge machine in which, ultimately, everything has to be explained in terms of unconscious and purposeless matter in meaningless motion.

Science assumes that the object is controlled wholly from the outside and defines it exclusively in terms of its external characteristics and relations. The evolution of a species, for example, has to be explained in terms of environmental adaptation or some other mechanism external to the species rather than, say, as the evolutionary thrust of consciousness needing more complex organisms for manifestation. This denial of any inner reality, however rudimentary, to a stone or a tree or an ape leads, with rigorous logical necessity, to the denial of such a reality—consisting of consciousness, purpose, intention, and conscience—to human beings.

Any notion of spirit as "pure consciousness" or of soul as a vehicle of "will" and "conscience" is, from a scientific point of view, unacceptable. One recourse from this materialization of human beings is to posit a sharp discontinuity between humans, specifically their minds, and the rest of nature. This is the path Descartes chose and many now follow. Such a sharp division appears to be, both from the philosophic and the scientific point of view, unnatural. If we proceed on the basis of a humanization or spiritualization of matter, we should expect different kinds of scientific theories.

Niels Bohr was right in his argument with Einstein when he said, "It is wrong to think that the task of physics is to find out how nature is. Physics concerns what we can say about nature" (Moore, *Niels Bohr* 406).

We adopt conventions according to their effectiveness in pursuing what we take to be the purpose and aim of the knowledge we gather. Convention and subjectivity are inherent in the much acclaimed objectivity of science.

At the root of the necessity to substitute intersubjective agreement for objectivity is the assumption that the knowing subject and the object of knowledge are inalienably distinct and separable from each other. It is an implicit assumption of the scientific revolution that the human cognizer is not a part of the nature being cognized; the person is separate from nature. This becomes more apparent when we confine our attention to a specific object of investigation, such as a molecule, a frog, or a star. Moreover, this separation is ensured by the experimental procedure.

The assumption of the separability of the subject and the object, which is a corollary of the presupposition that our self or identity is nuclear and localized in space-time, has a much longer history and wider base than modern science; one does not question it lightly. This may well be the area of greatest divergence between a rational and humanistic metaphysics, on the one side, and a mystical spiritual metaphysics, on the other. For the former, what is essential about each of us is our particularity and uniqueness, whereas for the latter particularity and uniqueness are secondary manifestations of a transpersonal reality. Since the alliance of Descartes and Locke, Western psychology has been basically atomistic, believing that a human being is primarily an isolated ego afloat in a sea of interactions, undulating in reaction to purposeless external forces.

Nevertheless, many artists, poets, and mystics have reported that, in their deeper experiences, the subject-object distinction is not as obvious and meaningful as it usually appears to our ordinary consciousness. They claim that the qualitative change they experience from separateness to oneness is the result of perceptions that are clearer and more heightened than usual. Some even say that taking the appearance of the knower-known dichotomy for reality is the very root of ignorance and that any observation in which the observer is distinct from what is observed is incomplete.

The suggestion is not that there is no distinction between the subject and the object at all and that an undifferentiated chaos prevails. It is, rather, that whatever is essential to the object—tree, poem, or person—is not comprehended as long as one stands completely apart from it, without participating in it, concerned only with the characteristics external to it. In any case, the rigidity of the subject-object distinction is not immune to doubt. If one gathered knowledge with a different purpose in view, one might see things differently; and the obviousness of our total separation from each other and the objects around us might well be like the obviousness of the sun's motion around the earth.

ABSTRACTION

The reality that is posited behind scientific observations is a mental construct and an abstraction (cf. chapter 4, "Western Science and Technology and the Indian Intellectual Tradition," in this volume). Scientific "reality" is not a matter of direct perception; it is a fabric of inferences, which in its turn leads to abstract generalizations forever subject to further reasoning and revision.

In the experiential approach to reality, as in some artistic and spiritual disciplines, the attempt is not to abandon the real phenomena that we perceive, by some kind of leap of reason, but to widen and sharpen our perceptions and to bring all our faculties to bear on what we experience. Theory is important here too, for obviously the reason that calculates and theorizes is also a perceiving faculty. But experience is more than theory; its significant features are immediacy, concreteness, and directness of perception. The point of theory is to help a person experience directly and fully. The point of experiment, on the other hand, is to lead to theory or to decide between one theory and another. In science, experiment has no meaning without theory; but in life, theory has no sense without experience.

This is as true of scientific theories as of metaphysical or theological ones; what is being called in question here is the tyranny of reason that makes theory superior to experience. For example, to theorize that behind the material world there is a spiritual reality is not essentially different from theorizing that behind the same material world there is a mathematical reality. Indeed, there are things which are mysterious; but the practical question is "How can I experience these?" rather than "What can I conjecture about them?"

What we seek in science, via experiment, is an abstract explanation of phenomena. What we might seek in life, aided by any theory, is concrete and experiential understanding of what is.

QUANTITY

One important feature of any scientific description is that it attempts to be quantitative. Most of the major scientists contributing to the scientific revolution appear to have been self-consciously opposed to the earlier, more qualitative, science. According to Galileo (*The Assayer*, in *Discoveries and Opinions of Galileo* 237–8):

> Philosophy is written in this grand book, the universe, which stands continually open to our gaze. But the book cannot be understood unless one first learns to comprehend the language and read the letters in which it is composed. It is written in the language of mathematics, and its characters are triangles, circles, and other geometric figures without which it is humanly impossible to understand a single word of it; without these, one wanders about in a dark labyrinth.

Similar enunciations were made by Kepler, Boyle, and Newton. It is not at all obvious, or even true, that to be mathematical means to be quantitative. Even the most apparently quantitative of all mathematical entities, namely numbers, cannot be considered without quality. Unity, duality, and trinity have qualitative aspects that are not exhausted by numerical manipulations. Nevertheless, in general, mathematization in science has meant quantification. According to the fathers of modern science, quantity is the fundamental feature of things, prior to other categories; in the realm of knowledge, quantity is the sole feature of reality.

Qualities, except insofar as they can be quantified, do not belong to what is real and cannot be avenues to truth. Exact science took a great leap forward when Isaac Newton in his *Principia* defined motion in terms of quantity of motion without regard to whether this motion was part of a sacred dance or a funeral march and when he defined matter in terms of quantity of matter without any consideration of where that matter belonged and what function it served. Unlike earlier natural philosophers, modern scientists do not consider qualitative aspects like place and function as being relevant to a precise definition of matter, motion, and other entities.

One cannot escape the impression that the prevalent general leveling down of quality and the pernicious reign of quantity—which has been passionately described by Ortega y Gasset in his *Revolt of the Masses*—is intrinsically connected with the scientific assumption that reality is primarily quantitative. Whatever functions painting, music, and dance may serve, when it comes to the serious business of truth and knowledge, as understood by modern natural philosophers, they are essentially frivolous. This is the seed of fragmentation of our sensibilities.

PERCEPTIONS

The scientific assumption about human beings is that they are essentially rational cognizers, and that everything else about them is secondary and capable of explanation in terms of their basic rational nature. This view of a person as primarily a passionless, disembodied mind, which would be recognized as the rigorously intellectual point of view, is shared by all who claim to be scientific in their professional work, from Descartes to the modern analytical philosophers. Other human faculties—feelings and sensations—are not considered capable of either producing or receiving real knowledge. It is no doubt true that, as we are, our ordinary sensory and emotional experiences are limited and subjective. In science, an attempt is made to minimize the dependence on such perceptions by agreeing that the corresponding aspects of reality not be considered as objectively real and by dealing with only those aspects to which rational constructs can be applied.

On the other hand, we might attempt to cleanse and deepen our perceptions so that we could see those aspects of reality that we ordinarily miss because we are oblivious to them, being preoccupied with our personal, subjective emotional existence, our fears and hopes, desires and wishes, likes and dislikes. This subjective preoccupation is the chief characteristic of the general state in which we ordinarily live. However, it is possible for a person to move in a clearer, more objective realm of feeling and then to engage this important aspect of oneself in perception, rather than to systematically eliminate it out of a suspicion, by itself well-justified, that our ordinary emotions are largely subjective and unreliable guides to truth.

Here, indeed, is an instance of throwing the baby out with the bath water. It has been bemoaned often enough that scientific knowledge does not address itself to the issues of human purpose and aspiration or to the meaning of human existence. All these concerns reside in feeling when it is a little freed from exclusively subjective preoccupations. Yet feeling is the one aspect of our wholeness rigorously ignored in the scientific methodology. It seems to have largely escaped modern epistemologists that feelings, when developed and trained, can yield objective knowledge. On the other hand, it is precisely through feelings, integrated with other faculties, that we can approach objective understanding, for feeling is the faculty of relation with any object; it is the reconciling aspect of human beings. Reason, on the other hand, differentiates, making distinctions and comparisons. If we make a fetish of detached rationality, we unnecessarily impoverish our perceptions.

CONTROL

Another basic assumption is implicit in the procedures and purpose of modern science, as distinct from that of ancient or medieval sciences. What modern scientists aim at is the prediction, control, and manipulation of what they investigate. Here is a statement by a Yale biophysicist, E. C. Pollard ("Mystery of Life" 7), discussing the adequacy of the laws of physics to explain the behavior of living organisms:

> The biophysicist approaches this problem by assuming that the laws of physics do work in the living cell and by putting together what information he has to try to predict how a given system should work. If the prediction proves correct, then presumably the present physical laws are adequate. If not, then perhaps new things will have to be found.

After noting some of the difficulties in investigating these matters, he adds:

> Eventually, of course, we'll surmount these obstacles, and then we'll know whether the cold laws of inanimate nature are enough to explain the nature of the living cell. If such should be the case, it will give us a control over the living cell which we have never had before.

Notice how easily words like "prediction" and "control" enter here as a matter of course. This is what "doing" means, the "doing" that is so intimately connected with scientific knowing—a point that has been well appreciated by the pragmatists and above all by John Dewey.

A question immediately arises concerning the reductionism involved in using the laws of physics to study living organisms, particularly human beings. Yet what is more pertinent here is something different, namely, the deep-rooted anthropocentric view of modern science, a view which, in the light of its own discoveries, could be considered absurd. It is certainly questionable that our relationship to the entire universe—in which we occupy a small place on an ordinary planet of a third-rate and peripheral sun in an average galaxy—should be primarily one of control. The spatial shift in the center of the cosmos, brought about by the Copernican revolution, appears to have been accompanied by a reverse epistemological shift toward a collectivized egocentricity in which human beings become the measure and end of all things.

What does this insistence on control and manipulation amount to in knowing something? Does it not guarantee that we cannot know, by these methods, anything that is higher than us, anything more subtle or more intelligent than us, if such a thing, or being, or force is not susceptible to our control? If scientists speak of lacking evidence of anything higher than human beings, that is to be expected, for their procedures specifically preclude the possibility of such evidence.

It can be argued that, even though the scientific approach might not be suitable for knowing anything higher than humans, it is nevertheless suitable for investigating nature. Even if this were the case, the arbitrary assumption clearly remains that nature is lower than humans neither encompasses us nor has any larger purposes. The tools used by science ensure the self-fulfillment of this assumption. This sundering of nature and human beings is very much a contribution of the scientific revolution, in particular of Descartes. It then becomes a matter of course that humans should want to conquer nature; a terminology of combat enters the scientific ethos without notice or comment.

If one succumbs to such an impoverished and partial view of nature, then one is forced to posit some notion of the supernatural to account for those manifestations, such as human will and purpose, that do not seem to be governed by completely unconscious mechanical laws. It is the high regard accorded to nature by thinkers like Spinoza and Goethe that got them into trouble with both the naturalistic scientists and the supernaturalistic clerics. Not infrequently, both of these tendencies coexist in the same person, as if a denigration of nature needs to be balanced by a deification of something extranatural, establishing rigid boundaries between various levels of being.

Scientific knowledge acquired by the imposition of this metaphysical straightjacket on reality is like a confession obtained under duress. Anyone who objects to such procedures is suspected by the contemporary intellectual orthodoxy of being opposed to reason and progress as well as of sabotage or defection to the enemy camp of hopeless romanticism or irrational mysticism.

Nevertheless, it is important to appreciate the magical spell of science for what it is. It would appear that whatever we can study from the scientific point of view of manipulation and control is something that can be compelled by us to yield answers to our questions. It cannot be higher than us; for that which is higher can be neither coerced nor violated by us. We can prepare ourselves for that which is higher and wait, actively making an effort of attention, observing without violence. This preparation and waiting for the revelation of the higher is not a passive affair, as it might seem. The activity involved in this state is of a sort quite different from the ordinary "doing" mentioned earlier.

Any vision of reality or any view of human knowledge that accepts fragmentation into compartments—such as the aesthetic, the scientific, the spiritual—is incomplete and productive of inner conflict and disharmony, which in turn result in external aggression and violence. The primary task of a sound theory of knowledge is to work toward principles and procedures that do not ignore any faculty of perception or any aspect of experience, thus maintaining the integrity and the wholeness of the investigators. Only then is it possible to ensure that the object of investigation will be understood as it is, rather than in conformity with a distorted sense of control and manipulation. There is no reason why we must behave like an appointed judge, compelling the witness to answer our questions, or like a pupil who is passive and subservient. We could, for example, approach reality sympathetically, neither aggressively nor passively, attempting to understand with the attention of all our faculties instead of a coercive reasoning.

The first principle of a theory of knowledge ought to be, not how we know something, but how we are to be with respect to it. The primary question is of our being rather than our knowing. If our assumptions and methods do not violate the integrity and wholeness of our own being, only then is it possible for us to understand something real about any object, without violence and distortion. In mentioning such a first principle, we have moved very far from the concerns and preoccupations of the metaphysics of science and of scientific philosophy.

No major Western philosopher since Thomas Aquinas—with the possible exception of the Cambridge Platonists in the seventeenth century—has considered the question of being as germane to the question of knowing. This is also the period of the rise and hegemony of the scientific mentality, which diminishes in both theory and practice all other human faculties than reasoning, and systematically ignores much of what makes us whole. Taking external experiment to be the sole criterion of knowledge institutionalizes a fragmentation of our sensibilities. Such knowledge cannot but work against the enlarging of being in humans.

Even in the disciplines where one might imagine that such questions have an obvious place, scientific procedures prevail, giving them a narrowly rational twist. Thus, to the extent that philosophy and theology become scientific, God is reduced to a mental construct: either a hypothesis for deduction or an inference from induction—in either case a construct for or against which one can have proofs or arguments, but of which one can have no experience. Theology thus becomes a rational profession dealing with metaphysical systems, rather than a psycho-spiritual path for the transformation of being.

Experimental knowing, because of the estrangement of the knower, is sundered from being and is concerned with a low order of "doing," involving control and manipulation. Experiential knowing, which now appears to be a different kind of knowledge—akin to gnosis, wisdom, or understanding—involves all aspects of humans and is intimately connected with the quality of being. Some of the ancients understood this, and Parmenides went to the extent of saying that "to be and to know are one and the same."

An exactly similar doctrine is found in Plotinus (*Enneads* 6.9). On the basis of such a theory of knowledge, in order to know something higher, one has to become higher. This is the central purpose of any spiritual tradition. The result of the scientific mentality in the realm of the spirit is to attempt to seize—as with drugs—higher consciousness. It is forgotten that if the spirit refers to anything higher than our ordinary self, the question is not how we can appropriate the spirit, but rather how can we prepare ourselves so that we may be appropriated by the spirit.

The concern for being, whatever else it involves, is a concern for the wholeness and integration of human beings, calling for a harmonization of the various faculties of perception. Only then can our different parts come together and act as a unified whole, enabling us to perceive openly, fully, and directly. This inner harmony of the soul is what Plato (*Republic* 443) considered necessary for just and beautiful action; and he regarded the knowledge leading to such harmony as wisdom. Clearly, no such inner synthesis and composure is possible without including our feeling perceptions. Science by systematically ignoring this side, has created a basic opposition to mysticism, which Goethe rightly called the dialectic of feeling.

A philosophy that loses sight of any one of the three major human concerns and necessities—namely being, knowing, and doing—is bound to be partial and self-defeating. By ignoring any one of these, we achieve knowledgeable action without compassion, or compassionate action without knowledge, or compassionate knowledge without action. The desirable alternative to the fragmentation and aggressiveness of science is not well-intentioned impotence or mystical passivity, but rather robust and integrated activity, without violence and without disassociation of our sensibilities.

Providing a sound critical basis for such theory and practice is important and urgent; otherwise irrational romanticism, for or against science, holds sway. Scientific commitment and the sensibility of wholeness are not inexorably opposed to each other; however, reconciliation is possible only when the partial finds its place in the whole; and reason, its place in being. Only when we proceed from an inner reconciliation can we hope to understand nature—its workings and its purposes—and cooperate in serving what is higher. Such knowledge can speak to our deepest aspirations and our search for meaning while revealing the beauty and mystery all around us.

IN THE BEGINNING IS THE DANCE OF LOVE

Our collective worldview, perhaps since the publication of Newton's *Principia* in 1687, has led us to regard questions concerning the origin, development, measure, and meaning of the cosmos as pertaining almost exclusively to the domain of science and in particular to that of physics. In other words, for us moderns, cosmology is a branch of physics, a subject that since the sixteenth century has concerned itself with understanding the cosmos ultimately in terms of dead matter in motion in reaction to external and purposeless forces.

Natural theology, however, has a long history. At the beginning of modern science, Kepler regarded himself as a priest of God in the temple of Nature. And for Newton, all his scientific work was a hymn of glory in praise of God. Since his time, scientists have felt increasingly uneasy about mentioning God, at least in their scientific publications. A long and hard struggle was necessary to establish natural science as an independent mode of inquiry, free of the tyranny of theology and the church, which had been coupled with temporal power. Now, especially since the making of the atomic bomb in 1945, it is science that is associated with power; and a similar struggle may be necessary to rescue genuine spiritual inquiry from the tyranny of scientific rationality.

A contemplation of the heavens has always played a significant role in bringing human beings to wonder about the meaning and purpose of the cosmos and of their own existence. The heavens have always seemed to be the abode of the sacred, inspiring reflection and awe. However, a subtle shift has taken place in our attitudes owing to the rise and development of modern science. Let us take a familiar example from Psalm 8, in which the psalmist asks:

> When I consider thy heavens, the work of thy fingers,
> the moon and the stars which thou hast ordained,
> what is man, that thou art mindful of him?

We too have contemplated the heavens and other things in the light of the latest scientific knowledge, but our attitudes, and our questions, are different. If I may be permitted a modern rendering of the psalm, the scientist is more likely to ask:

> When I consider the heavens, the work of our equations,
> the blackholes and the white dwarfs, which we have ordained,
> what is God, that we are mindful of him?

Ideas and activities flourish and change in the context of a worldview, although worldviews themselves are permeable and elastic. Science is the major component and the strongest constituent of the present paradigm, and all our intellectual discussions now take place in the assurance of a shared scientific rationality.

I do not have any new data to bring for consideration of the question "Origin and Evolution of the Universe: Evidence for Design?" And I do not really believe that what we need, collectively or individually, is additional data to come to a proper sense of a design or its absence in the cosmos, and of our relationship with it. What I propose to do is to raise some issues and make some comments about and around the theme of this question, organizing my discussion under subheadings conveniently provided by the key words of the question: *origin*, *evolution*, *universe*, *evidence*, and *design*. These terms conform to a particular kind of rationality and circumscribe our deliberation of the question.

ORIGIN

The question of the origin of the universe is intimately connected with the understanding of time. It is practically impossible for the Western mind, particularly since Augustine in the fifth century, not to think of time linearly. The notion of linear time has entered deeply into the structure of scientific thinking. Even when we think of nonlinear time, as we sometimes do in contemporary physics, we look at the nonclassical properties of time: what its conjugate variables are, how it works in other dimensions and spaces, and so on. But it is important to emphasize that in physics we are always dealing with some dimension of time, and never the sort of situation when "time shall be no longer" (Revelation 10.6). Of course, when we extrapolate along the dimension of time, we might run into a singularity, as we do for example in the equations dealing with gravitational collapse or the cosmological solutions leading to the big bang theory of the origin of the universe. There our notions of time go awry, and we need some very ingenious methods to get around these difficulties.

The thing to note, however, is that from the point of view of physical cosmologists, the questions concerning the beginning of the universe have to do entirely with smaller and smaller amounts of time from the initial event when all this began. However many theoretical or practical difficulties we might encounter, what in fact we are trying to do is to follow the time coordinate back to zero. We have theories now dealing with the state of the universe at time spans of the order of 10^{-23} seconds after the absolute zero of time. There are theoretical reasons for believing that this may be the closest we can get to the absolute beginning along the time coordinate. If so, according to our present notions of time, it makes no sense to talk about time any closer to that beginning and certainly not prior to it.

The sort of beginning that the physical cosmologists search for is not, however, the beginning spoken of in the mystical or the mythical literature. When it is said, for example, in the opening lines of Genesis, "In the beginning God created the heaven and the earth," we are tempted to think that according to the Bible the heaven and the earth were the first manifestations. To do so, however, is a mistake, as we see from the immediately following verses. The heavens were not created until the second day and the earth not until the third; and the heavens, also called the firmament, were created in order to divide the waters above from the waters below. These waters, one should notice, existed before the existence of the heavens and the earth, which, on the other hand, were said to be created in the beginning. Perhaps we are presented with two different kinds of heavens and two different kinds of earth. I shall not engage in biblical exegesis here; all I wish to suggest is that we have here a notion of a beginning that is different from the scientific notion.

Of course, in such passages, we may be encountering difficulties with language that are endemic to all religious literature, often also to poetry, as well as to almost any situation of intimacy. But there is no reason for us to imagine that the scriptures are meant to be at our service and that they must be clear to us while we remain as we are. I imagine that, at the least, scriptures summon us to realities that we do not ordinarily perceive. There is universal agreement among all spiritual traditions that, for us to perceive these hidden realities, something in us needs to change. We cannot remain as we are and come to the Mystery. That change is called by many names: a change in the level of being, a change in consciousness, a deepening of faith, a new birth, the opening of the third eye, the true gnosis, and so on. One of the fundamental changes that is said to occur when the doors of perception are cleansed concerns time: Not only does one's sense of duration change but, more important, one's relationship with the passage of time alters radically.

Statements like "In the beginning was the Word" are not statements concerning ordinary time, the sort of time on a coordinate axis whose point of origin is the beginning. These statements carry weight and significance precisely because they were uttered and received in heightened states of awareness. It is true that scriptures can be and have been misused to cover up intellectual laziness or to foster fear, hatred, bigotry, and the like. Such misuse can make a spiritual document or symbol fearful and even hateful to people of goodwill. Nevertheless, whenever these writings and symbols speak to anyone spiritually, it is because they carry a higher level of energy and not primarily, or even at all, because of any logical clarity or agreement with our scientific notions of space and time.

This other kind of time, that of myth and mystical writing, is certainly not contradictory to our ordinary time. Nor is it, however, merely an extension of it—in either direction of the time coordinate, to the beginning or to the end. Just as the scriptural "beginning" is not the zero of the time coordinate, so mystical "eternity" is not an infinite extension of time. Thus what is everlasting is not necessarily eternal. It appears that spiritual time is in a way orthogonal to scientific time, in the sense that mathematicians use the notion of orthogonality, which is to say that it lies in a dimension wholly independent of the domain of time, although it is able to intersect with time at any moment. Thus, even if we were to consider time multidimensionally, or even nonsequentially, or any other way, no manipulations of time or in time could lead to the dimension of eternity that is orthogonal to it and that speaks of mythic beginnings and endings.

Evolution

As long as there is time, there is change. That is how we understand and measure time; that is how we know that time exists and that it passes. It is only in this minimal physical sense, of state A changing into state B, that we speak about the evolution of the universe in physical cosmology. But there is an ordinary use of the word *evolution* that has a certain emotional connotation of which we need to be careful; otherwise we only introduce a philosophical problem where we do not intend to. Ordinarily, one thinks of evolution as containing within it an idea of change in a desirable direction, so that the end product is at a level higher than the antecedents.

Now, it is very difficult to say in what sense one understands "level." There are some connected notions like development, growth, and progress. Something or someone who is at a higher level may have more being, more consciousness, more wisdom, or the potentiality to perform more complicated tasks than one at a lower level. What is important is that the idea of hierarchy is built right into the notion of levels and of evolution, and that, furthermore, we specify which we view as higher or lower, or whether a process is degenerative, progressive, or static. What cosmologists really talk about is physical change, without attaching any notion of hierarchy of being. But once the universe unfolds, it may be judged from a particular point of view. As in the Genesis account of creation, at the end of each day and each new manifestation, God looked at it and pronounced it to be good. Our cosmologists consider what they think happened and pronounce the change to be evolution. All that our physical laws describe is change in time. There is nowhere any place in them for intention, purpose, or evolution as long as it contains the emotionally laden sense of progress.

It is worth paying a little more attention to this point. In the history of natural philosophy, ideas relating to change and the laws governing the dynamics of nature have been intimately connected with notions of causality, and for obvious reasons. Three distinct notions of causality can be distinguished for our purposes: metaphysical, physical, and biological.

The metaphysical notion of causality, which prevailed until the sixteenth century, assumes that the cause is greater than the effect. Thus, in theology, the creator is naturally greater—at a higher level of being, intelligence, and power—than the creation. This principle was applied also in natural philosophy and was, from the point of view of the subsequent developments in science, a stumbling block to a proper understanding of nature.

During the sixteenth century, a new understanding of physical causality emerged, according to which the cause and the effect were at the same level. This was a time in history when there was a general leveling off in every field of human culture and society. In natural philosophy one did not speak of a cause being higher than, or in some senses containing, the effect. Instead, one spoke of the change of one state of matter into another, without raising or lowering its level of being or intelligence or desirability. The sixteenth-century shift from metaphysical to physical causality was a subtle one, from the domain of intentions, will, reasons, and purposes, and the forces and laws required to carry out these intentions in nature (or, in another language, from angels and powers), to a field of forces and laws operating in nature without any purpose. The philosophical and theological controversy between Leibniz and Newton was connected with this shift in the understanding of causality and the consequent sundering of the realm of facts from the realm of intentions, or of nature from spirit.

In the nineteenth century, a biological notion of causality emerged, according to which the cause is lower than the effect. That which is inferior, ontologically or in intelligence or in the subtlety of cellular organization, gives rise to what is superior. Thus amoebas would give rise, in time, to Einstein. Since what follows is more desirable than what precedes, from the human point of view, this notion of causality is rightly called evolution. This principle is the inverse of the metaphysical and the theological notion of causality: Rather than proceeding from above, creation—including human beings—now proceeds from below. In its wake, this idea naturally brings an immense amount of anxiety and unease, especially to those who are comforted by a belief in some ultimate cause, or God, who is personally concerned about their welfare.

Returning now to scientific cosmology: It is only in this century that the idea of the entire universe itself being dynamic was formulated precisely. One of the solutions to the field equations of General Relativity demanded that the universe as a whole be dynamic; otherwise the solution was unstable. This notion of the dynamism of the cosmos seems to have been such a revolutionary idea in the Judeo-Christian world that even a radical thinker like Einstein balked at it. He tinkered with his equations and introduced another factor into them, called the cosmical constant, which was helpful in obtaining a stationary solution to the field equations. Soon after, it was discovered that even with this new, somewhat arbitrarily introduced, constant, dynamic solutions of the equations still resulted. Also, within a few years, Hubble discovered from observational data that the galaxies were receding from each other at the speed of light and that the universe was therefore expanding. This was the most significant observational confirmation of Einstein's theory of General Relativity, and Einstein himself later remarked that the introduction of the cosmical constant in his field equations was "the greatest blunder" of his life.

Thus the fundamental equations on which modern physical cosmology is based have nothing to do with evolution, except in the minimal physical sense of change. Modern cosmology is just like the rest of physics as far as the notion of causality is concerned: it describes the change in matter-energy from one state to another. Naturally, from our point of view, the emergence of the stars, galaxies, the solar system, and ultimately of ourselves is more desirable than their nonemergence, and so we feel justified in describing this change as evolution.

We need to be aware that in this process we are combining two different notions of causality described earlier. One of these we actually need for our knowledge; the other is an emotional overlay for the obvious reason that we humans are at the end of the corresponding change. So we get saddled with a philosophical problem because of our sentimentality about human beings while nevertheless insisting on a limited physicobiological view of man. We do not need so limited a view of cosmology that the deepest, spiritual part of ourselves cannot be taken into account.

In physical cosmology, which is a perfectly legitimate and wonderful study in its domain, it is change in the physical form of matter-energy that is our concern. We do not speak, indeed we cannot speak within the assumptions and procedures that govern the subject, of spiritual evolution. Of course, human beings have always had a need and a sense of the sacred; this alone gives meaning and purpose both to ourselves and to the cosmos. Fundamentally bereft of the sacred, we are riddled with personal anxiety and adrift in the meaningless vastness of space-time. Physical theories concerning the static or the dynamic nature of the universe are not, nor do they pretend to be, about significance or purpose.

UNIVERSE

What do we mean by *universe*? Presumably, all there is. Does a cat or a bee have the same universe as a human being? Does a tone-deaf or a color-blind person have the same universe as the one who is musically gifted or is a painter? Does a person who is blind to symbols or to spirit, or who is insensitive to wonder, beauty, or spiritual presence have the same universe as a scientist or a poet or a mystic?

What there is, is a function of who sees. This axiom is not meant to support the philosophical position that claims that a thing does not exist unless someone sees it. My concern is our knowledge: What we know, actually and potentially, about the universe depends on the procedures, methods, and interests that we bring to our observation of it. If we do not know how to find angels and we are not interested in them, we will say that the angels do not exist. And it is true that they are not a part of our scientific universe. Nor are "the clouds which brood," which were a part of Wordsworth's universe, nor are the dancing colors inhabiting Blake's universe, nor are the cherubim and the seraphim singing "Holy, holy, holy," who were a part of Bach's universe. The physical cosmologist's universe, vast and marvelous as it is, is not all there is. As Shakespeare would have put it, "There are more things in heaven and earth than are dreamt of in your philosophy."

Even when allowance has been made for error and illusion, which can, of course, as much blight the cosmologist as the poet, the musician, or the mystic, it is difficult simply to dismiss these other fields. Hardly anyone of sound judgment and goodwill dismisses the arts out of hand. But it is astonishing that many people find it much easier to dismiss the mystic and the theologian. There are understandable historical reasons for this dismissal, but what concerns us here is that in intellectual circles none of these fields are now considered relevant to deliberations concerning the cosmos.

The universes the artist, the musician, or the mystic regard as most precious, we relegate to a murky and imaginary realm, not entirely real. We think those imaginary realms are certainly not as real as the multiple universes or the shadow universe or the anti-universe or the other weird universes that make up the speculations of contemporary physical cosmologists. We assume that whatever musicians, artists, or mystics might be doing, they are certainly not producing knowledge. Knowledge is produced exclusively by scientists, we would say, and by nobody else. And contemporary philosophers, with all their love for wisdom, in general agree. We might not now say, with the positivists, that "nonscience is nonsense," but we would surely say that nonscience cannot lead to knowledge and truth.

What we include in the universe is related to a traditional idea of "levels of materiality." Medieval philosophers held that the matter on different planets was different, as were the laws in operation there. It was a considerable advance in astronomy to establish that fundamentally the same sort of matter prevailed throughout the universe, subject to the same laws everywhere. However, when we move from medieval natural philosophy—whether alchemy, astrology, mathematics, or cosmology—to the modern sciences, our general reaction to the backward-looking nature of the past and our excitement over new discoveries blind most of us to the predominantly symbolic and analogical nature of medieval thought.

There is an ancient analogy between each human being and the universe, between the microcosm and the macrocosm, which inwardly mirror each other's essential principles. We might then realize that the various planets, the different materials on them, and the different laws operating there were all symbols of different levels of interiority within a human being, and that the quality of matter-energy at different levels of the mind is different from the matter-energy of the body and subject to different laws. Sometimes this idea was explicitly shown in various diagrams, but the prevalence of symbolic and analogical ways of thinking meant that it was often just assumed, much as we today assume that everyone in all reasonable gatherings naturally accepts the mode of scientific rationality. It is plain and obvious; as Blake succinctly put it, "Reason and Newton are quite two things." What goes on in our minds and our feelings, and not only what takes place in our bodies, also contributes to all there is.

Mental and psychic functions are not in principle outside the domain of scientific knowledge. They are not supernatural, as opposed to natural, and thus excluded from the investigations of natural philosophy. There is nothing supernatural about most of what gets labeled extrasensory perception or miraculous. Extrasensory perceptions, to be sure, are at present extrascience perceptions, but there is nothing inherently beyond nature or beyond science in them. It may well be that a radically altered science will be required to understand what is now called extrasensory perception, just as a radically altered science was required to understand lightning in the sky or the light of the sun, which might have seemed quite supernatural from the perspective of fourteenth-century scientists. It is important to distinguish, as St. Augustine did, between what we claim really is nature and what we know of nature. The limits of our knowledge are not necessarily the limits of nature.

But it is still more important to realize that, even with a radically altered science that could take account of extrasensory perceptions and other "miraculous" happenings, we cannot come to the end of all there is. "All there is" far exceeds the realm of nature, the domain of causality and materiality, however subtle our descriptions. To say that we do not yet know certain levels of nature is not to say that nature is all that there is to know or that can be. In fact, practically without exception, all great spiritual teachers, such as the Buddha, the Christ, Patañjali, Krishna, and Moses, have warned against an excessive fascination with miraculous phenomena and occult powers, which are said to be diversions from the true spiritual paths.

Two related, although somewhat parenthetical, remarks may be made here. The first remark concerns an important distinction, made in the scientific revolution starting in the sixteenth century, between the primary and the secondary qualities of matter. This distinction played a crucial role in the development of the physical sciences and also in the subsequent impoverishment of nature. The primary qualities were extension, mass, and velocity; to this list was added charge in the nineteenth century and spin, strangeness, charm, and others in the twentieth. The secondary qualities consisted of taste, color, smell, and the like; they were not considered objectively to be a part of nature, but were subjective and rather unreliable. Considered even more subjective and unreliable were tertiary qualities, feelings of beauty, purpose, or significance.

The secondary and tertiary qualities were gradually eliminated, not only as instruments of inquiry into nature, but also as fundamental constituents of nature. They could not, properly speaking, be studied as themselves constituting reality, but as something that needed to be explained and understood in terms of the primary qualities. Thus a deep-seated reductionism is built into the fundamental presuppositions of scientific inquiry. A division into *res extensa* (what can be measured) and *res cogitans* (what is aware) carried within it a certain instability attached to the realm of the mind. From a scientific point of view, as we see clearly in behavioral psychology, all psychic functions must be reducible to external motions.

On the other hand, we have the philosophical problem of mind-body dualism. In some theological circles it is really understood as soul-body dualism, in which the soul is supernatural, removed from the realm of nature and scientific investigation altogether, and placed in the realm of faith, away from knowledge. Any real knowledge of the psyche or the soul thus gets rather short shrift: The scientists deny the existence of anything in it that they cannot study by physical means, and the theologians deny the possibility of any knowledge of it. But in neither case can spiritual qualities have any independent existence in the cosmos that we can study.

The second, related parenthetical remark derives from a comparative study of the history of ideas in the Western world and in India. In Greek philosophy and in the early Christian writers, as well as in the Indian tradition, there was a tripartite division of a human being into spirit, soul, and body, or, to use the terminology of St. Paul, *pneuma*, *psyche*, and *soma* (Armstrong and Ravindra, "Dimensions of the Self "). Gradually this threefold division shrank into a twofold division: spirit and nature, or mind and matter, or soul and body. Descartes explicitly identifies spirit with soul and both with the mind. In the Western world, since the time of Descartes, soul is in general regarded more or less completely as spiritual rather than natural.

A partial reduction of the threefold division into a twofold one took place in India as well. However, there, in general, the psyche has been considered in the realm of nature, and therefore subject to the laws of nature and amenable to scientific inquiry. Thus thoughts and feelings, and psychic phenomena, including those considered paranormal, are in the realm of *prakriti,* nature—that is to say, in the domain of materiality and causality. According to Indian thought, the so-called miracles, for example those mentioned in the Bible, are not supernatural or spiritual, even though they are unusual and extraordinary. Spirit is still beyond.

EVIDENCE

We have already spoken about the somewhat obvious fact that our knowledge depends on the procedures, methods, and interests that we bring to knowing the cosmos. Neils Bohr was quite right in saying that "It is wrong to think that the task of physics is to find out how nature is. Physics concerns what we can say about nature" (Moore, *Niels Bohr* 406). Of course, even what we can say about nature depends on the mode of discourse a community of scientists accepts as appropriate. In that universe of discourse, only certain kinds of data are acceptable as evidence, and certain other data are not acceptable. For example, the angels, so very real to Blake, are not acceptable scientific data, nor are Bach's fugues. In fact, no interior experience is a part of scientific data.

Scientific knowledge is not a knowing-by-participation, but a knowing-by-distancing. It is not an I-thou knowing but an I-it one. Thus we see that scientific knowledge is indeed objective; but it is not objective in the mystical sense, in which the observing self is so completely emptied or "naughted" that the object reveals itself as it is, the thing in itself, in all its numinosity and particularity. Sages in all cultures have said that it is only in this state of consciousness, devoid of the self, that an object is known both in its oneness with all there is and in its distinct uniqueness. An entity—a tree, a person, a culture, or the whole cosmos—is then understood both in its interiority and its externality, including its generality and specificity. Scientific "objectivity" comes from another route, even in the etymology of the word (from Latin *obicere*, "to throw in the way, to hinder"), when we throw ourselves over and against something, as is understood in our word *objection*. One mode is love; the other, combat.

Mystics are constantly speaking about love. We are told that God is love, as in the New Testament, or that love is what supports the whole cosmos, as in Dante's *Divine Comedy*, or that love was the first creation and absolutely everything else came from it, as in the Rig Veda. But by our scientific methods we wish to conquer nature as if she were an adversary. In fact, scientists almost never refer to nature as "she"; they always call her "it." Naturally, what is dead or was never alive can hardly have intentions, purposes, reasons, or feelings. In short, it can have no interiority. Evidence that involves this sense of interiority, that is based on an I-thou relationship, is out of the scientific arena altogether.

What is at issue here is a different sort of knowing. The important thing is not to see different things, but to see things differently; not changed or expanded contents of the same consciousness, but a different quality of consciousness. Just as one can be in an I-thou relationship with even a cat or a tree, as Martin Buber used to say, one can also bring the I-it attitude to human beings, or even to God, if we seek only to use them as objects. Such, for example, was the attitude of Newton, perhaps the greatest of all scientists; as one of his biographers, Frank Manuel, has remarked, "For Newton, persons were usually objects, not subjects." Scientists have no monopoly on the I-it attitude, nor are they, as a class, devoid of the I-thou intercourse. But when they are doing science, scientists automatically exclude the I-thou attitude and any observations based on the interiority of the object from the body of scientific evidence.

In the last four centuries, there has been a virtual explosion in the number of scientific instruments that have extended our ability to observe the very small and the very far away and to measure extremely small amounts of time. Because of this immense quantitative expansion of the field of our observation, we now see the cosmos with different eyes. There has been an extension, but not a cleansing, of our eyes, as Blake or Goethe would have understood it. Nothing in the nature of science itself might lead us to invoke, with St. Francis, "Brother Sun; Sister Moon."

Any of us—scientists as well as nonscientists—can, of course, be deeply moved by a sense of our oneness with the cosmos. Furthermore, anyone can be struck by the wonder, the mystery, and the design of the cosmos as much today as in the days of Newton or Archimedes or Pythagoras, although unfortunately most of us are all too rarely struck in this way. These feelings and perceptions lie in dimensions different from the ones in which our scientific observations are extended. No amount of quantitative expansion of data and theories can lead to the dimension of significance, any more than an endless extension of time can lead to eternity.

DESIGN

It is hard to imagine a scientist who does not see order in the universe, a harmony of the various forces that permit the continued existence of the world, and a pattern involving regularity of phenomena and a generality of laws. The more we know about the universe, the more elegantly and wonderfully well-ordered it appears. Most scientists share with Einstein (*Out of My Later Years* 26) a "deep conviction of the rationality of the universe," and his feeling that no genuine scientist could really work without a profound "faith in the possibility that the regulations valid for the world of existence are rational, that is comprehensible to reason." Einstein himself called this a "cosmic religious feeling," which he regarded as the "strongest and noblest motive for scientific research." Even though other scientists may be shy or embarrassed by the word religious, they are by no means strangers to the feeling that Einstein is describing.

What puts scientists on guard is not the idea or the feeling of "design" in the universe, but a suspicion that, lurking behind the slightest concession in using the word, is a theologian who will jump with glee and immediately saddle them with the notion of a Designer and all that goes with it. It is not the design that the scientists are uneasy about, but the designs that they smell hiding behind the slightest admission of it! It is no use telling them that the theologians have been on the defensive now for nearly three hundred years and are so eager to gain any approval from their scientific colleagues that they get a little overenthusiastic if they sniff any possibility of truce.

All of science is a celebration of pattern, regularity, lawfulness, harmony, order, beauty; in other words, all the marks of design. What it does not have much to do with is the Designer, who is over and above the design, occasionally interfering in the universe in contravention of natural laws. Already in the seventeenth century, Leibniz was able to remind Newton that his God was like a retired engineer: Having created perfect laws and having set the universe initially in motion, He was no longer needed and could be on a permanent sabbatical. The very perfection of scientific laws and their comprehensibility make the continued presence of this sort of God less necessary.

To have to infer the Designer from the design is largely a particular type of theological and linguistic habit. It is based on a notion of design that is more technological in character than scientific or artistic. In art there is always present a definite element of play, improvisation, and surprise. No creative work is like painting by numbers; the artist does not know beforehand what the finished product will be like. And any scientist who already knows what he is going to find at the end of his work does not need a research grant, for he hardly needs to carry out the research. I am not discounting the intuitive conviction that a scientist can have about a particular idea or a method, so that he knows prior to engaging in a detailed calculation or an experiment what the outcome must be. But every good scientist, even an Einstein or a Newton, has many intuitive convictions that just do not lead anywhere. In the actual working out of the ideas and their encounter with what is, is the real delight, excitement, and even terror of creativity. Without them, scientific and artistic activity would be very dull.

And any God who might create the universe without delight, without playfulness, without wonder, and without freedom and fresh possibilities would be a very dull God indeed. He would be a God of grim specialists, but not of the dilettantes, those who delight in what they do and study. Such a God could be a good technician carrying out a technical design, or a good bureaucrat keeping everyone in his place, or a thorough accountant keeping track of everyone's actions for later dispensation of necessary judgments; he might even make a good president of a large corporation like a modern university. But he certainly would not make a good scientist, artist, or mystic. Such a God could not be the God of love or of wisdom, and it would be very difficult to take delight in Him.

Etymologically, *design* is related to *sign from*. Sign from whom? Historically, in Christian theology, with rare exceptions, the signs are always from a personal God. However, there are profound and fundamental incompatibilities between scientific knowledge and the idea of a personal God, in spite of the fact that many very great scientists, for example Newton, were deeply committed to a personal God. Here is a brief excerpt from a manuscript of Newton, now in the Jewish National and University Library (*Yehuda Ms.* 15.3, fol. 46r):

> We must believe that there is *one God* or supreme Monarch that we may fear and obey him and keep his laws and give him honor and glory. We must believe that he is the father of whom are all things, and that he loves his people as his children that they may mutually love him and obey him as their father. We must believe that he is *pantokrator* Lord of all things with an irresistible and boundless power and dominion that we may not hope to escape if we rebel and set up other Gods or transgress the laws of his monarchy, and that we may expect great rewards if we do his will . . . to us there is but one God the father of whom are all things and we in him and one Lord Jesus Christ by whom are all things and we by him: that is, but one God and one Lord in our worship.

However, since Newton's time, and at least partly owing to the very science he took a major hand in creating, scientists are much less comfortable about accepting such a faith in a personal God, and certainly in expressing it. There is a feeling of a fundamental incompatibility between science and such a faith. Most scientists these days are likely to agree with Einstein in his description of what he called his religious feeling as one of rapturous amazement at the harmony of natural law, which reveals an intelligence of such superiority that, compared with it, all the systematic thinking and acting of human beings is an utterly insignificant reflection. The most beautiful thing we can experience is the mysterious. It is the source of all true art and science. To know that what is impenetrable to us really exists, manifesting itself as the highest wisdom and the most radiant beauty which our dull faculties can comprehend only in their most primitive forms—this knowledge, this feeling, is at the center of true religiousness. In this sense, and in this sense only, I belong in the ranks of devoutly religious men. (*Ideas and Opinions* 11)

Many people who knew Einstein personally insisted that he was the most religious person they had ever met. But he was not religious in any church or denominational manner. As he said, many times and in many ways, "My religion consists of a humble admiration of the illimitable superior spirit who reveals himself in the slight details we are able to perceive with our frail and feeble minds. That deeply emotional conviction of the presence of a superior reasoning power which is revealed in the incomprehensible universe forms my idea of God" (quoted in the *New York Times* April 19, 1955, obituary).

Here we see a very good illustration of the fact that being struck by the beauty, harmony, order, and design in the universe does not necessarily mean accepting a personal or a sectarian God. It is worth quoting Einstein at some length on this point, from a remarkable address on "Science and Religion" at a symposium in 1941:

The main source of the present-day conflicts between the spheres of religion and of science lies in this concept of a personal God. It is the aim of science to establish general rules which determine the reciprocal connection of objects and events in time and space. For these rules, or laws of nature, absolutely general validity is required—not proven. It is mainly a program, and the faith in the possibility of its accomplishment in principle is only founded on partial successes. The more a man is imbued with the ordered regularity of all events the firmer becomes his conviction that there is no room left by the side of this ordered regularity for causes of a different nature. To be sure, the doctrine of a personal God interfering with natural events could never be refuted, in the real sense by science, for this doctrine can always take refuge in those domains in which scientific knowledge has not yet been able to set foot.

But I am persuaded that such behavior on the part of the representatives of religion would not only be unworthy but also fatal. For a doctrine which is able to maintain itself not in clear light but only in the dark, will of necessity lose its effect on mankind, with incalculable harm to human progress. In their struggle for the ethical good, teachers of religion must have the stature to give up the doctrine of a personal God, that is give up that source of fear and hope which in the past placed such vast power in the hands of priests. In their labours they will have to avail themselves of those forces which are capable of cultivating the Good, the True and the Beautiful in humanity itself. This is, to be sure, a more difficult but an incomparably more worthy task. (*Out of My Later Years* 28–9)

In my judgment, which in this regard is different from Einstein's, the major cause of the incompatibility between science and theology or church religion, which should certainly not be confused with spirituality, is not so much the concept of a personal God as the restricted view of knowledge that prevails in scientific circles, as remarked earlier, and the limited notion of the Spirit or Divinity that the theologians have. To have understood rightly that Divinity is at least at the level of the human person does not mean that it is only personal. The personalist aspects of Being, such as intelligence, intention, will, purpose, and love, which are all marks of interiority, do not have to lead to a concept of a personal God made in the external image of man, with definite form and being separated from others. Uniqueness of any level of being, seen separated from the oneness of all Being, leads to a limitation of vision, to partiality, and to exclusivism.

As the scriptures tell us, human beings are made in the image of God, which I take to mean that a human being is potentially able, in the deepest part of self, to be one with the Divine. This is what the sages have always said, everywhere, whether the expression is *aham brahmāsmi* or "My Father and I are one." However, if we forget the summons for an inward expansion to God, we are bound to reduce God in an outward contraction to human beings.

Concluding Remarks

I have suggested that there is more to the universe and to knowledge, and the corresponding evidence, than is encountered in physical cosmology; that there are dimensions of the existence and development of being other than in time; and that one can be very spiritual with a personal God or without one. These are practically truisms. My observations have nothing to do with being Eastern or Western. Of course, one is conditioned by one's cultural background. However, the more deeply one delves into oneself, the more one discovers one's common humanity with others, and one's commonality with all there is, without thereby losing one's uniqueness. In this necessary realization of our oneness as well as uniqueness, we may, each one of us, have to travel paths we do not ordinarily travel, in lands we do not usually inhabit, and experience modes of being not habitually ours.

Different modalities and levels of being, and the corresponding levels of thought and feeling, exist in every human being and even more so in every culture. Some contingent, historical factors can overwhelm or underscore a particular modality at any given time. The tremendous impact of science and technology in the West in the last two centuries has made some modes of being now appear to be non-Western. Yet we are now in a particularly exciting situation of a global neighborhood demanding a larger vision of ourselves. A special kind of insensitivity is now required for us to remain culturally parochial, refusing to become heirs of the great wisdom of mankind: as much of Plato as of the Buddha, of Einstein as well as Patañjali, of Spinoza no less than of Confucius.

A major conceptual revolution was created in the Western world when the works of Aristotle were discovered by the Latin West through the Arabic philosophers in the eleventh and twelfth centuries. That revolution went on for several centuries, leaving no area of thought and culture untouched. It appeared for a time that the major synthesis brought about by Thomas Aquinas between Aristotle and Christian thought was a culmination of this revolution. But no, it rolled on until and including the major scientific revolution of the sixteenth and seventeenth centuries that was finally brought to a close by Newton. Since the end of the nineteenth century, we have been in the middle of another very major encounter of different cultures and different streams of thought, of the West with the East. There is, moreover, an important aspect of the contemporary situation since the Second World War: for the first time in history major cultures are juxtaposed as neighbors without being in the position of either the victor or the vanquished. Who knows where the resulting cultural revolution will end?

One thing, however, is certain: A consequence of this revolution is bound to be a recognition, in addition to the experimental science of nature, which has been a particular achievement of the modern West, of an experiential science of the spirit freed from all sectarian theology. This science of the spirit is not the same thing as an extension of our present science to include occult phenomena and extrasensory perceptions. Also, one should not let oneself be seduced by superficial parallels between certain expressions and paradoxes of contemporary science and ancient Oriental thought. It is true that here and there are beginning to appear, in the long column of Western appellations in the honor rolls of science, names like Chandrasekhara Venkata Raman, Tsung Dao Lee, Hideki Yukawa, Abdus Salam, and Chen Ning Yang. In his day, Kepler was convinced that the Sun was the Father; the circumference of the solar system, the Son; and the intervening space, the Holy Ghost. A latter-day scientist, brought up on different symbols and metaphors, might see in the patterns appearing in the cloud chamber the dance of Shiva, or be moved to find in the complementarity appearing in the quantum phenomena yin and yang encircled together, or discover the resolution of the various paradoxes of contemporary physics in the ineffable Tao. These parallels or interpretations are as true or false now as they were then. They add nothing, either to true science or to true spirituality.

There is a deep-seated need in human beings to seek an integration of all their faculties, and a unity of their knowledge and feeling. We are fragmented and thirst for wholeness. This thirst, however, cannot be quenched by mere mental conclusions and arguments about the parallels between physics and Buddhism or about the existence and nature of the design in the cosmos. What we need is a radically transformed attitude in the deepest sense, which would permit us to receive true wisdom and intelligence from above ourselves, and to use our science and technology with compassion and love. Without this attitude we cannot reconcile Blake and Newton, and their heirs. And the lament will continue:

> O Divine Spirit sustain me on thy wings!
> That I may awake Albion from his long and cold repose.
> For Bacon and Newton sheathed in dismal steel, their terrors hang
> Like iron scourges over Albion, Reasonings like vast Serpents
> Infold around my limbs, bruising my minute articulations.
> In heavy wreathes folds over every Nation; cruel Works
> Of many Wheels I view, wheel without wheel, with cogs tyrannic
> Moving by compulsion each other: not as those in Eden: which,
> Wheel within Wheel, in freedom revolve in harmony and peace.
>
> (William Blake, *Jerusalem* 15.9–20)

The tension between the two major contributing streams to the Western mentality, the Greek and the Hebraic, with their respective emphases on the cosmological and the theological perspectives, is very old. Whitehead once remarked that this tension may have been the main source of the creative dynamism of the Western culture for centuries. However, now there is almost a complete separation between these two perspectives. Scientists are deeply committed to the cosmological perspective to the exclusion of the person.

On the other hand, neither theology nor philosophy has been an experiential science for many a century. If we were to take the corresponding experience seriously, as with great mystics and spiritual masters, one thing would become immediately clear: There is not much meaning to consciousness or intelligence, and thus to God, without the accompanying attributes of action, love, and delight. These are not so much attributes of the spirit, added from the outside and without which the spirit could exist, as they are the means by which we recognize the presence of the spirit or consciousness or intelligence.

Thus God is not only omniscient, but also omnipotent, omni-amorous, and omnidilettante! This is precisely what makes the spirit omnidelectable so that human beings are constantly drawn to her and are in love with her. Occasionally, they write poems of ecstasy for the spirit, as did Alexander Skryabin, a Russian composer and poet of the early twentieth century in his "Poem of Ecstasy":

The Spirit playing,
The Spirit longing,
The Spirit with fancy creating all,
Surrenders himself to the bliss of love.
Amid the flowers of His creation, He lingers in a kiss.
Blinded by their beauty He rushes, He frolics, He dances,
He whirls.
He is all rapture, all bliss in this play
Free, divine, in this love struggle
In the marvelous grandeur of sheer aimlessness,
And in the union of counter-aspirations
In consciousness alone, in love alone,
The Spirit learns the nature of His divine being.

Thus the design and the intelligence in, behind, and above it turn into a dance. Some dancers come and go, join the dance, or stop to watch it; but the dance goes on eternally, in the beginning as now, in love and delight. In moments of wholeness, of deep feeling and clarity of awareness, each dancer is both unique and one with the cosmos, knowing that in the beginning is the Dance of Love.

TO THE DANCER BELONGS THE UNIVERSE: FREEDOM AND BONDAGE OF NATURAL LAW

THE CHALLENGE OF BEING HUMAN

There are over six billion of us on the surface of this planet. Over six billion human beings, like you and me, each one with aspirations and regrets, fears and ambitions, memories and hopes. We all have our occasional grand philosophical moments—in the midst of much longer periods of uncertainty, hesitation, and habitual repetition. And each one of us occupies a place in a gargantuan funeral march, each day moving closer to the exit by steady steps. Between now and a year from now, a hundred million of us will die: A hundred million sparks of consciousness will be extinguished, some barely sparking, some ablaze in glory, but each one coming to a definite and discernible end.

However, life and consciousness will continue to assert themselves, and a hundred million or more centers of awareness, with fresh memories and new hopes, will be born. This cycle of life, which includes both the being born and the dying, has continued for hundreds of thousands of years, creating an astounding variety of human beings, each one completely unique and yet each one quite replaceable in the mammoth Dance of Life. Dancers come and go, but the dance continues. Each new beat of the drum presents to time new faces to see, as the old ones disappear from view. No wonder that in the myths of so many ancient cultures the Earth is spoken of as the Great Goddess with an extremely fecund womb and a very destructive jaw, producing and devouring at the same time.

What meaning has this Great Dance of Life? Perhaps that is too large a question to raise now. So, let us ask, what place do we human beings have in this Dance? First of all, collectively as humanity, What role do we have in the cosmic economy? Biologists, especially marine biologists, have very clear ideas about the role and function of almost every animal in a large-scale ecological chain. They can tell us, for example, how kelp is needed for the lobsters to grow, how the sea urchins are also necessary in this chain, except when they become too abundant, and so on. Every creature has its place and function so that the whole ecosystem can flourish. So we may rightly wonder: What function has humanity? What do we contribute to the smooth and harmonious working of the system of the Earth? We depend on the Earth; but does the Earth need us? Does the Sun? This is not a new question; as long as humanity has existed, the awareness of the vastness of the universe has made human beings aware of their smallness and has raised questions about their place. A familiar example is Psalm 8, cited earlier:

> When I consider thy heavens, the work of thy fingers,
> the moon and the stars, which thou hast ordained,
> what is man, that thou art mindful of him?

Our contemporary idiom may be a little different, as is our knowledge about the solar system and the far-from-central place the Earth occupies. We know that we live on a quite mediocre planet moving around a peripheral and third-rate star in an average galaxy. But we also wonder about our place in this largeness. There are immensely vast stretches of time and of space, and humanity exists like an excrescence confined to a few meters depth on the skin of the Earth. What is humanity in the midst of this immensity? No one can fail to appreciate the vastness, intricacy, and delicacy of the whole structure of the universe. The physical and chemical characteristics, not only of the environment on the Earth, but also of the cosmos as a whole seem to be artfully and finely tuned, with humanity precariously balanced in a state of extreme fragility. Consequently, one cannot but endorse the cosmic feeling of awe that Einstein (*Ideas and Opinions* 40) described as one of "rapturous amazement at the harmony of natural law, which reveals an intelligence of such superiority that, compared with it, all the systematic thinking and acting of human beings is an utterly insignificant reflection."

It is a consequence of this amazing harmony of natural law that we are here, that a hundred million of us die every year and a hundred million or more are born. We are not here contrary to law. We may not know the precise mechanism by which we came to be, and we may not know the function we have in the vast universe. There may be enough uncertainty about all this that some of us may declare ourselves to be here by random chance, just as some thinkers have been driven to conclude that the universe is chaotic and absurd because they could not make sense of the events around them.

Making an exception for such desperation, it is hard to imagine a scientist who does not see order in the universe, a harmony of the various forces that permit a continued existence, a constant unfolding of the world, and a pattern involving regularity of phenomena and generality of the laws. The more we know about the universe, the more elegantly and wonderfully well-ordered it appears. Most scientists share with Einstein his "deep conviction of the rationality of the universe," and his feeling that no genuine scientist could really work without a profound "faith in the possibility that the regulations valid for the world of existence are rational, that is comprehensible to reason" (*Out of My Later Years* 26).

Einstein himself called this a "cosmic religious feeling" that he regarded as the "strongest and noblest motive for scientific research" (*Ideas and Opinions* 39). Even though other scientists may shy from the label "religious," they are by no means strangers to the feeling described by Einstein. What is essentially at issue is the fundamental lawfulness of nature. This is not something that can be proved by scientific research; this is a philosophical and psychological prerequisite for such research.

Of course, at any stage of development of scientific thought, the precise range and applicability of a given set of natural laws may undergo a radical revolution, as happened for example in the establishment of quantum mechanics, by which the laws turned out to be statistical, applying to ensembles of particles rather than to individual particles. But we do not abandon the idea that there are laws of nature. That idea is needed for us to think coherently about nature and to communicate our thoughts to each other.

Returning to our initial question about the place of we human beings in the lawful Dance of Nature, but now individually: What is my place? Why am I here? What am I? Maybe humanity in the large has some function to play in the ecology of the earth, but what about me personally? Am I completely replaceable in an ensemble of human beings as far as the vast cosmos is concerned? What meaning is there to my individual existence? What is the significance of my personal hopes and aspirations?

What was said several thousand years ago by a poet in the Rig Veda (1.164.37) can be said by any one of us: "What thing I am I do not know. I wander alone, burdened by my mind." This burden of the mind, this wandering alone in inquiry, this passion for knowing what one is and how one is related to the cosmos, is peculiarly human. Inhabiting a dying animal as we all do, each one of us is nevertheless condemned to question and search for self-awareness.

Concern with such eternal questions is what gives the great spiritual documents of humanity their abiding quality. But they have more than questions: They point to another level of consciousness, another mode of existence, towards which we could aspire, and where questions about our individual and collective significance can come to rest and find some resolution.

The hymn of the Rig Veda continues: "When the Firstborn of Truth has come to me I receive a share in that selfsame Word." How do I prepare to receive the Firstborn of Truth, which elsewhere in the Rig Veda is said to be Love? How do I dwell and participate in the Word, which is from the Beginning? Some readers will recognize echoes from the first chapter of the Gospel according to St. John. Using a metaphor from that gospel one may ask: Lambs of nature as we are in any case, how can we also become lambs of God?

TRANSFORMATION AS A HUMAN IMPERATIVE

In asking questions about how we can be or become, we are asking about the possibility of transformation from one level of being to another. We are unfinished creatures, and the world is incomplete and unfinished along with us. However well balanced and ecologically sound the universe may be without our human interference, we seem driven by our deepest internal necessity, possibly in fulfillment of a requirement of the cosmos, not only to understand the cosmos but also to transform it. We cannot be human unless we intervene in the natural order—both inside as well as outside us. Human beings are creatures who must intervene; they cannot leave themselves or the cosmos the way they find them.

By "transformation" I do not mean "change." All the changes brought about by human intervention do not necessarily lead to transformation either of human beings or of the cosmos. Everything in the universe is constantly undergoing change; that is how we measure time. Change is a truth and law of nature; it is natural. Transformation, on the other hand, is intentional change; it is not natural. All works of art are examples of transformation. To bring into existence a sculpture from the material of a stone needs the intentional intervention of a human being. We are constantly called to make ourselves, the Earth, and the whole universe into works of art.

For the transformation of a human being, in what the alchemists called the Great Work, great art is needed. To live and die as a lamb of nature is natural. But to live and die as a lamb of God is not natural; it requires a teaching, a spiritual path, effort, and grace. The transformation from one kind of lamb to another requires intentional change; it is brought about by art and the corresponding skill and hard work. In the Sanskrit language, an ordinary person, as one is born and lives, is called *prakrita*, which means natural, vulgar, common, unrefined. But, those who are able to intervene in their internal cosmos and are properly educated can be transformed into *samskrita:* well made, refined. They are not wholly controlled by their natural inclinations; they are not completely determined or bound by natural law.

Each one of us is an artist of our own life: starting from the raw material of our self, we sculpt something from it which corresponds to our aspirations, our understanding, the level of our engagement, our skill and sensitivity. We wish to become more rightly aligned; even our most superficial good manners indicate a wish for right internal and external order; and the most dedicated social climber among us nevertheless expresses a wish for larger and freer being. What we make of ourselves depends not only on our own abilities and work, but also on the various forces assisting or hindering us. But we must engage in the work of transformation; this is an imperative of our human existence.

TWO NATURES

We need to be careful and to avoid the pitfalls that we can anticipate. The first difficulty lies in the use of the words "nature" and "natural." In saying that transformation is not natural, I do not mean to suggest that it is artificial in the pejorative sense of that word. I mean rather to say that it requires art and work and will not be done automatically by itself. Another way of saying this is that human beings have a purpose to their existence; they are needed in the cosmos. A human being fulfills this purpose when engaging in the work of inner and outer transformation.

We may distinguish "purpose" from "function" in the same way as "transformation" from "change," namely by the necessity of intentional intervention. Whatever our function in the scheme of nature—it may simply be to produce a certain amount of carbon dioxide for the trees, to add to the humus in the soil or to produce food for the worms—it will in any case be performed automatically in response to natural forces, as are the functions of kelp and lobsters. As we are born, breathe, procreate, and die, we fulfill our natural function, whatever it may be. The hundred million who die this year fulfill this natural function.

The fulfillment of our purpose, however, needs an active participation on our part, a certain degree of choice and intention. This is what gives meaning and significance to our lives. Our function could be fulfilled collectively and interchangeably by one person for another; but the accomplishment of our purpose requires a unique engagement by each one of us. We may not know what our purpose in life is; or even when we sense what it is, we could still fail in the fulfillment of this purpose; and we could refuse to engage with it at all.

Perhaps not quite. It does seem that some human beings, and the most sensitive and creative among us belong to this group, are unable to refuse to engage with the whole complex of purpose, meaning, significance, and transformation. They are condemned to it, and cannot deny it without denying their own humanity. They have an internal daimon, as Socrates had, which drives them, or they are compelled by the Muse, or they are hounded by God, as was the case with practically all the prophets in the traditions of Judaism, Christianity, and Islam. At least in their cases it seems more accurate to say that it is a part of their nature that compels them to struggle against other parts of themselves to do what they must, in response to what they recognize as their higher urges.

In fact, it is commonplace in many ancient traditions to speak in terms of two natures of human beings, often labeled "higher nature" and "lower nature," frequently in conflict with each other, one concerned with purpose and the other with function, possibly symbolized by the vertical and the horizontal dimensions of the cross. To make the distinction between the two natures clearer, we should recall that sometimes their tendencies are called "spiritual" and "natural."

All these labels have their difficulties, especially when they are considered without reference to any experiential data, as is generally the case in philosophy and theology. What we need is a superscience, a science of the higher nature or of the spirit, a science dealing with the whole arena of purposes and significance and the transformation of being and the laws pertaining to them. This superscience would be one in which actual experience has an important place in validating or refuting the theories, statements, and claims. This superscience would deal with human beings not only as they ordinarily are, but as they could be.

We do not have any commonly accepted name for such a science at present. We might use "numenology" (the science of spiritual presence) or "autology" (the science of the Self) to convey some idea about the sort of inquiry it is. Older labels, such as "theology" (the science of the divine) and "ontology" (the science of being), although by themselves wholly appropriate, will no longer now do because they have been co-opted by sectarian and exclusively mentalistic enterprises without reference to any objective experience.

In spite of the difficulties associated with the label "higher nature" for the spiritual aspect of a human being, it has one great advantage. We are used to the idea that there are laws in nature, that there is causality, that there is a possibility of inquiry and investigation. And this inquiry needs to take into account higher-order laws, it needs to make room for human intention and purpose; nevertheless, it is an empirical inquiry and not something accepted without experiential investigation and reference to objective experience.

"Objective experience" is not exclusively or even necessarily external. That is why this superscience has to be fundamentally different in its assumptions, procedures, and goals from other natural sciences that have attempted to model themselves after physics for the last three centuries. At the present time, no interior experience is a part of scientific data, especially of physics, a subject that since the sixteenth century has concerned itself with understanding the cosmos in terms of dead matter in motion in reaction to external and purposeless forces.

The objectivity of the natural sciences can relate only to those aspects that can be externalized. All aspects of interiority, such as intentions, purposes, and significance—all the aspects that easily come to mind when one speaks about the higher nature of human beings—are left out.

The usual scientific knowledge is objective in many senses, but it is not objective in the mystical spiritual sense, in which the observing self is so completely emptied that the object reveals itself as it is, the thing in itself, in all its numinosity and particularity. As sages in all cultures have said, only in this no-self state of consciousness is an object known both in its oneness with all there is and in its uniqueness. Any entity—a tree, a person, a culture, or God—is then understood both in its essential interiority and in its wholeness, including generality and specificity. Such is the state of insight described as truth-bearing *(ritambhara)* in Patañjali's *Yoga Sūtras*, the classical text of Yoga.

In another cultural metaphor, he who can be so completely emptied of himself that he could say, "I am not myself the source of the words I speak: it is the Father who dwells in me doing His own work" (John 14.10), can speak authoritatively both of the uniqueness of the Father as well as of oneness with Him (Ravindra, *Christ the Yogi*). For him there is no contradiction between these two statements, which are both objectively true: "The Father and I are one" (John 10.30) and "The Father is greater than I" (John 14.28).

The fact of two natures in us is a matter of experience and cannot be denied. Too bad for any system of thought that does not make room for both of these. We ought not deny one or the other, nor assume that they are the same or that one is reducible to the other (Ravindra, *Whispers from the Other Shore*). The two natures are born of different parentage: each of us is born of human parentage, but it is possible, according to all spiritual traditions—even though their precise metaphors and nuances are quite different from each other—for a person to be born again of divine parentage, "begotten not by blood, nor by carnal desire, nor by man's willing, but by God" (John 1.13). This birth of an inner being is a virgin birth because it is a spiritual birth without any carnal intercourse.

Whether we speak of two natures or two beings in us, spiritual and physical, where the physical includes the mental and the emotional, we cannot escape the fact that these two beings follow different laws, the law of spirit and the law of flesh. There are teachings, for example in Tibetan Buddhism, in which inner birth is spoken of in terms of several subtler bodies arising from the gross body by alchemical transformation of substances. St. Paul also has fragments of this doctrine. The point to be emphasized here is that, just as there are levels of physical and mental development within the lower nature, similarly there are levels of development in the spiritual nature; and different laws, permitting different degrees of freedom, apply to different levels.

SPIRIT, SOUL, AND BODY

There is a saying *(hadith)* attributed to the Prophet of Islam. Upon returning from a battle, Prophet Mohammed said to his disciples, "We have returned from the little holy war to the great holy war." When the disciples pressed him for clarification, he said, "The little holy war is a war against the infidels, but the great holy war is the war against one's own soul."

In the Christian world of modern times, "soul" is considered to be so wholly good and spiritual that the idea of waging a war against it is likely to sound like siding with the devil. But in many ancient traditions— and certainly in early Christianity, Greek philosophy, and Indian thought—a developed or mature human being was regarded as having three distinct parts: spirit, soul, and body, or to use the New Testament terminology of St. Paul, *pneuma*, *psyche*, and *soma* (Armstrong and Ravindra, "Dimensions of the Self"). In this division, *pneuma* (spirit) is suprapersonal, manifesting itself in or through a person or in other ways, whereas *psyche* (soul) belongs to the person. Thus it makes sense to speak of "my soul" but not of "my spirit." On the other hand, one can speak of "the spirit" or of "the spirit in me."

Returning to the saying of the Prophet Mohammed, the war against the soul, in the context in which it is spoken, is a war against one's own lower nature. Similarly, Jesus Christ says several times (Luke 14.26, for example) that he who does not hate his psyche—which is to say his soul or self—cannot be a disciple of his. Soul there, as in Indian thought, belongs to the lower realm. However, within this lower realm (also spoken of as the realm of the "world" or of the "flesh") lie the possibilities of a new life, a birth into the higher world of the spirit.

In a threefold division of a human being, which is philosophically clearer and more satisfying than the twofold one, the struggle between the spiritual and carnal natures is waged in the human psyche. In the play of forces in one's own soul, a human being can side completely with one or the other side, becoming wholly an animal or an angel, or one can keep both of them in their proper balance and be truly human. A properly ordered person does not deny the body-mind, but is not driven by it. For a rightly aligned person the body-mind is like a horse for the spirit to ride, needing to be disciplined as well as befriended but certainly not to be brutalized. To use a classical analogy: The spirit has the vision, but is lame; the body-mind is blind, but can carry and move. Together they can constitute an integrated and whole person—with both the vision to see what needs to be done and the ability to carry out the corresponding action.

DIFFERENT LAWS FOR DIFFERENT LEVELS

At the level where most of us live, practically all our behavior and everything else about us is completely determined by ordinary laws. At higher levels of spiritual development, which require an intentional intervention and are by no means automatically accomplished in nature, one develops increasingly those aspects of being that are free of the lower laws and subject to the higher laws. Whether we follow the essentialist metaphor, as used in most religions, and say that we can discover our deepest spiritual Self or God which is already in us, or whether we follow the existentialist metaphor so that a person has to create this spiritual part, the important point is that some purposeful action, an intentional undertaking, is required from human beings. Speaking in a religious mode, even as we see that without God it cannot be done, we also see that without human action it will not be done.

However, not everything in a developed human being becomes free of the usual laws of birth, change, and decay. The physical body still obeys the laws of its own level; but one discovers or creates and progressively lives from a more subtle part of oneself that itself is relatively freer of the laws to which the body is subject.

Only at the highest possible inner development of a person could one say that the most spiritual part—God, the Absolute, Brahman—is beyond all laws and is therefore completely and absolutely free. But this is like a theoretical limit, where our mental concepts break down, as in dividing a number by zero, and we need to be extremely careful about extrapolating from that sort of a limit to anything practical. Whereas it may be true to say in some cases, for example for Jesus Christ when he is one with God, that for them the law is ended, still that does not mean that there are no laws in the realm of the spirit.

The spiritual and the natural realms may be distinguished by different sorts of laws, but they are not separated by an abundant lawfulness in the one realm and its absence in the other. There may in fact be more of a continuity in practice between these realms than is allowed by theoretical theology, which has brought in its wake disastrous consequences wherever it has prevailed. On the one hand, it has cut off the spirit from the bodily center of human beings in the natural rhythms of life; on the other hand, it has fostered an opposition between natural science and spiritual life. Above all, it is spiritual life that has suffered by losing touch both with the body and with the intellectual principles of empirical inquiry.

The fact that so far, while speaking about the two natures, spiritual and carnal, our attention has been confined to human beings should not blind us to the possibility that these two realms exist even in the cosmos, with different laws, containing many gradations within them, and that the whole creation participates both in materiality and spirituality. All creatures and constellations, however brutish and solidly material they may be, have the possibility of consciousness, even if only at a rudimentary level. Also, there was a well-nigh universal idea throughout the ancient and medieval worlds that a developed human being is a microcosmos mirroring inwardly in essential principles the large cosmos, and vice versa.

The presence and action of subtle spiritual energies and beings, variously called angels, devas, gods, fairies, and spirits, are globally attested. The fact that we cannot detect these with our ordinary scientific concepts and instruments does not mean that they do not exist, as observed in chapter 8. The physical cosmologist's universe, vast and marvelous as it is, is not all there is. Spiritual realities cannot be seen with ordinary eyes or their extensions at the same level; a new being and a transformed vision are needed for their apprehension. As Plotinus said (*Enneads* 1.6.9), "to any vision must be brought an eye adapted to what is to be seen, and having some likeness to it. Never did eye see the sun unless it had first become sun-like, and never can the soul have vision of the First Beauty unless itself be beautiful."

In a science of higher nature, a mind with steady attention and a heart cleansed of egoistic cravings may be the greatest scientific instruments. What can be perceived by a person with a disciplined body, steady mind, and clear heart, in other words, a third-eye universe, is quite different from what can be seen by the two ordinary eyes and their quantitative extensions. We do not need more and more things to see with the same eyes; what will really affect us is to see, even the same things, with different eyes.

NEW PHYSICS AND HUMAN FREEDOM

There is something particularly sad about the eagerness with which many so-called religious people have latched on to one or another discoveries or theories of modern physics to justify their faith or to find some room for their religious positions. Before the sixteenth century in Europe, every activity had to be justified in the light of Christian theology, just as for decades in the twentieth century in the USSR, everything had to be justified in the terms of dialectical materialism. In the Western world for a couple of centuries now, and increasingly in the rest of the world as well, the true intellectual orthodoxy is that of science. If you want to sell anything or promote anything, it is better to have science prove its value—

whether it is a particular kind of toothpaste or transcendental meditation. Every guru feels a little more secure if a scientist, especially a physicist with a Nobel Prize, is also sitting on the dais! Now even God has to be scientifically acceptable. Our modern attitude is better reflected in the following reworking of the verse from Psalm 8 quoted in chapter 8:

> When I consider the heavens, the work of our equations,
> the blackholes and the white dwarfs, which we have ordained,
> what is God, that we are mindful of him?

What do we expect science to do for us? What do we hope from it? Wisdom? Freedom? Salvation? Can any discoveries or creations of science bring about a transformation of our own inner being, where alone true freedom and bondage lie? Can any theory or external authority do this for us? For that matter, even in the realm of the scriptures, whose total concern is with salvation or enlightenment, what will knowledge of them do? Are the theologians saved—those who have studied all the influences that shaped the scriptures? Are the physicists enlightened—those who can solve the latest conundrums in magneto-geometrodynamics? What is it that we need? It surely must reflect a peculiar kind of psychological uncertainty to require a bolstering by the up-to-date findings of quantum mechanics, or to be assured of free will by them. Did the Buddha have to wait for the proof of Bell's theorem or the theory of relativity or holography? Is next year's Nobel Prize winner in physics more unified or whole than Kepler or Pythagoras?

If we are totally out of touch with our own center, we can have no inner orientation; then the sense of ourselves needs to be supported by the changing theories in science or in theology. This kind of external prop can substitute for the discipline of an actual inner search and block a real centering of oneself. The more we rely on mental constructs rather than a direct seeing of ourselves, the farther we get from our own inner essential core, or from the *hara* where Zen satori takes place, or from the belly from where the rivers of living water flow according to Jesus Christ (John 7.38). Einstein was right when he said, "The present fashion of applying the axioms of physical science to human life is not only entirely a mistake but has also something reprehensible in it" (Planck, *Where Is Science Going?* 209).

Schroedinger was even clearer: "Physics has nothing to do with religion. Physics takes its start from everyday experience, which it continues by more subtle means. It remains akin to it, does not transcend it generically, it cannot enter into another realm" (Schroedinger, *Science, Theory and Man* 307–8). He characterizes such attempts as "sinister." "The territory from which previous scientific attainment is invited to retire is with admirable dexterity claimed as a playground of some religious ideology that cannot really use it profitably, because its [religion's] true domain is far beyond anything in reach of scientific explanation" (Schroedinger, *Nature and the Greeks* 8).

Also, we should not let ourselves be seduced by superficial parallels between certain expressions and paradoxes of contemporary science and ancient Oriental thought. They are entirely different from each other in their procedures, intentions, goals, and consequences simply because they deal with two different kinds of nature (cf. chapter 3, "Perception in Yoga and Physics," in this volume). Furthermore, these parallels are, in general, pressed by people who, although they themselves derive from the Judeo-Christian traditions, yet have very little sympathy with the principles and idioms of Western spirituality, which they regard to be fundamentally different from Oriental spirituality.

Any true science of the spirit must rely on the perceptions and understanding of transformed human beings so that the levels of reality which are generically and qualitatively different from the ones now studied by the natural sciences can be apprehended. Such sacred sciences have existed for centuries as Yoga, Zen, alchemy, certain aspects of Sufism and of monastic Christianity, but often they have fallen into sectarian and acquisitive hands. A consequence of this has been that the bright minds and sensitive hearts in the modern age have shied away from them. As this science of the spirit is freed from an exclusively sectarian, rationalist, and obscurantist hold, it will be more and more appreciated for its true value in enabling people to discover and fulfill their unique purposes.

The greatest discovery of modern science is the discovery of its own limitations, and an increasing appreciation of the fact that what we know depends not only on what is out there but also on who we are and how we see. Our knowledge cannot be separated completely from the nature of our being and the quality of our attention. Corresponding to many levels of being within ourselves, from the totally determined to the most free, there are many levels of knowledge.

Not all levels of knowledge are at present included under the rubric of science, but that is not important. What is more important is that there be a practical inquiry into transformation of a human being from being a slave of fear and ambition to becoming free. Natural science can help this inquiry but it can also hinder it, depending on what relationship we have with science. But, whatever science may discover, whatever social or political conditions may prevail, the cultivation of inner freedom cannot but be undertaken by an individual, in the arena of one's own soul. There a person must struggle with those parts of which are frightened by the possibility of genuine transformation and which would barter away real freedom for self-importance.

Natural Law as a Foundation for Freedom

All ancient traditions believed in the lawfulness of the universe and in the corresponding bondage imposed on human beings by nature and her laws. From a philosophical and spiritual point of view, there is nothing new about the so-called problem of determinism versus free will; it has not arisen since the successful application of Newtonian mechanics to the solar system; nor has any radically new light been thrown on it since the development of quantum mechanics. Determinism of an effect by a cause is a notion that is integral to the concept of law. If there is lawfulness, there is determinism.

But, also—and this needs to be emphasized—precisely because there is lawfulness, there is the possibility of freedom. A law also indicates the payment required for freedom from that law. Space travel would have been impossible without understanding the law of gravitation, which keeps us tied to the earth. To travel in space, we must know precisely what escape velocity is needed to overcome the effect of the law of gravitation in a particular situation, and we must have the requisite fuel and technology to acquire that velocity. It is only a romantic notion to imagine that we can acquire immortality, salvation, or freedom for ourselves without making the requisite payment exacted by the law that keeps us naturally and quite lawfully enslaved. Of course, everywhere in the world some form of religion can be found that will sell some cheap indulgences, physical or doctrinal, to unsuspecting buyers and try to assure those who are gullible that they are specially chosen for grace now and glory in the hereafter.

Returning to an example of natural law, we can look at the law of causality, applicable to all nature, internal and external, and enunciated in many cultures in one form or another for millennia. In India it is expressed as the law of karma. Confining our attention to human beings alone, we can express the law of karma as follows: As one is, so one acts; and as one acts, so one becomes. It is like the mutually interactive system of space-time and matter in the theory of General Relativity: Matter affects space-time and space-time affects matter. In the law of karma, being affects action and action affects being.

If I am a certain kind of person, I would naturally find myself doing certain sorts of actions. In their turn, these actions that I perform leave grooves of tendencies on my being, altering it so that I become a certain kind of person. At the next opportunity, I will act in accordance with these tendencies of my being, my future action (karma) thus being determined by my past action. Major actions leave deep impressions in the psyche, creating knots in it that affect my future actions for a long time without my being necessarily aware of the knots or their initial causes.

As a general principle, the effects of karma are not restricted to only one lifetime; the law cuts across the boundary of what is ordinarily called life and death. It may be remarked parenthetically that action here does not mean simply bodily activity, but also includes thoughts and feelings and intentions. If I think bad thoughts about anyone, not only does that reflect the quality of my being, but it also further affects this quality.

This is an example of a traditional law of nature, understood more or less in this form by the two thirds of humanity now residing in Asia, and in any case by the vast population in Hindu and Buddhist countries. This law is a law of determinism; but it is also a law that makes freedom possible and provides the basis for any spiritual practice. Understood partially, from the point of view of only one level within a human being, the law of karma creates a vicious circle from which one cannot escape, and it has quite often been understood in this manner, leading to despair and resignation.

However, when viewed from the perspective of a whole person, the law of karma can indicate to those willing to undertake the discipline involved in the cleansing of their perceptions precisely what the knots are in their lives that compel them to act the way they do, even against the will and understanding of their right mind, and also how to resolve and overcome these knots.

More important, a person can depend on the law of karma and undertake a spiritual striving in the assurance of the knowledge that the universe or the gods do not act capriciously and that no one is going to be elevated or degraded accidentally. Each one of us is responsible for our life—even to the final extent of salvation or perdition—and the dignity of our human existence and action is founded on the solidity of a law working in every part of the cosmos.

In correspondence with our own deep-seated spiritual urges, each one of us has the possibility of making efforts in order to overcome the compulsions of the lawful and natural workings of our own tendencies, which are based on our past experiences, knowledge, and impressions. This is the meaning of spiritual striving, a struggle against our own determined nature, in which the spiritual aspects of the cosmos help the spiritual aspects of humanity, just as the unintentional and natural parts of the universe aid the unintentional and natural existence of human beings.

Freedom Not for Oneself but from Oneself

As has been remarked, it is intentional intervention that transforms human beings so that they not only perform a natural function in the cosmos, but also have the possibility of fulfilling a spiritual purpose. What makes this intentional undertaking possible is attention. This is the reason why in all spiritual teachings—the *Yoga Sūtras*, the Philokalia, or Zen practice—attention in its various qualities and levels constitutes the main instrument of transformation.

Attention freed from egoistic fears and ambitions, which are constantly turning the mind to the past and the future dimensions of time, taking it away from the present moment in which alone the dimension of eternity intersects that of time, is the essence of serious prayer and meditation. These in turn are the ways of connecting with the higher parts of oneself and of the universe and with the corresponding higher laws, rather than being petitions for the suspension of laws in special cases.

The spirit is discovered or created with attention founded on a progressive clarity of the mind and the heart. From the grossest level of being to the most subtle, all levels are reflected in the quality of attention and the corresponding degrees of freedom. The creatures most bound are the sleepiest, with only instinctive attention. At the highest level, the freest attention, or the purest seeing, is what constitutes wakefulness and spirit.

The basic existence of the spiritual self has to do with attention, sensitivity, mindfulness, intention, and insight—the very qualities that make us truly human and truly free. But these are not the qualities that are automatically acquired in nature; they all require effort, education, work, and, in general, a spiritual path involving an enormous struggle with the worldly forces within oneself that are fueled by fear, ambition, and egocentricity.

Freedom is thus not an actuality for a vast majority of human beings, who have neither the inclination nor the ability to struggle against their own lower natures. However, it remains a potentiality for all those who have cultivated themselves properly. Ordinary human beings are in fact quite determined by their cultural, social, and psychological conditioning, in reaction to which arises self-will. Those who live wholly from self-will are completely determined by their past actions and reactions, ricocheting down the corridor of time, without ever being able to engage in a fresh action, in the present moment of eternal now, in which alone there is real freedom. As the *Theologia Germanica* (chapter 34) says, "Nothing burneth in hell except self-will." And what is hell, if not the prison created by a totally determined ego?

Free human beings, on the other hand, by no means do "their own thing." They realize that freedom is not in opposition to law or order—that would be just anarchy and chaos—nor even in spite of the law, but because of it. Freedom is grounded in the law; those who do not respect the natural law—both the inner and the outer—cannot be free. Freedom is possible only when a person is internally rightly ordered, so that the lower and less conscious parts are able to hear and obey the more conscious parts. Certainly in the spiritual context it can be said that perfect freedom arises only from perfect obedience, a complete submission of self-will to the order inherent in the vastness or the Tao.

The ultimate payment exacted by the law of freedom is the sacrifice of one's egoistic self, of all the parts which are bound and unconsciously repeat compulsive actions determined by the past, which gives one self-importance and the impression of having a purpose isolated from that of the cosmos. Those who can pay the price of self-sacrifice can be free. That was the case of Jesus Christ, who thoroughly emptied himself and died to his self-will, so that he could be filled with the being and the will of God, and say on the eve of his death that his joy was now complete.

According to the *Yoga Sūtras*, sages come to final freedom when their insights are in accord with cosmic order, so that their conflict and sorrow are ended. Such persons are not free *for themselves*, but free *from themselves*, from the part of the self that is willfully isolated from the laws, purposes, and intentions of the vastness. Freed from the burden of the self, and from regrets about the past and anxieties about the future, such a person is able to be present here and now and to dance. A dancer is freest when naturally in harmony with the tempo and the rhythm of the dance. Then, the dancer belongs to the universe and the universe belongs to the dancer, mutually supporting the fulfillment of each other's purpose.

SCIENCE AS A SPIRITUAL PATH

Science is the paradigm of knowledge for us moderns. What does this knowledge tell me about myself? About my place in the cosmos? About the point of my being? About the direction of my knowing or the sense of my doings?

Science leads to, and perhaps presupposes, not only a physical cosmology, but also a psychological and an existential cosmology. How is scientific knowledge related to the spiritual aspect of human life? Is it completely tangential? If it is, why bother with science? With respect to what does science have any significance?

Does science have any spiritual significance? It seems logical to address this question first of all to scientists, and among them the greatest. What motivates them in their searches? Albert Einstein, in an address given in honor of Max Planck, said:

> In the temple of Science are many mansions, and various indeed are they that dwell therein and the motives that have led them thither. Many take to science out of a joyful sense of superior intellectual power; science is their own special sport to which they look for vivid experience and the satisfaction of ambition; many others are to be found in the temple who have offered the products of their brains on this altar for purely utilitarian purposes. Were an angel of the Lord to come and drive all the people belonging to these two categories out of the temple, it would be noticeably emptier, but there would still be some men, of both present and past times, left inside. . . . If the types we have just expelled were the only types there were, the temple would never have existed, any more than one can have a wood consisting of nothing but creepers. Now let us have another look at those who found favor with the angel? What has brought

them to the temple? That is a difficult question, and no single answer will cover it. To begin with, I believe with Schopenhauer that one of the strongest motives that leads men to art and science is escape from everyday life with its painful crudity and hopeless dreariness, from the fetters of one's own ever-shifting desires. A finely tempered nature longs to escape from personal life into the world of objective perception and thought; this desire may be compared with the townsman's irresistible longing to escape from his noisy, cramped surroundings into the silence of high mountains, where the eye ranges freely through the still, pure air and fondly traces out the restful contours apparently built for eternity. (*Essays in Science* 1–2)

In these remarks about Planck, Einstein is of course also revealing his own motives for pursuing science: a longing for freedom from merely personal life and a search for the world of objective perception and thought. Towards the close of his life, while writing a brief autobiography (which is remarkable in its paucity of personal material), he said:

Even when I was a fairly precocious young man the nothingness of the hopes and striving which chase most men restlessly through life came to my consciousness with considerable vitality. . . . By the mere existence of his stomach everyone was condemned to participate in that chase. Moreover, it was possible to satisfy the stomach by such participation, but not man in so far as he is a thinking and feeling being. As the first way out there was religion, which is implanted into every child by way of the traditional education-machine. Thus I came . . . to a deep religiosity, which, however, found an abrupt ending at the age of 12. . . .

It is quite clear to me that the religious paradise of youth, which was thus lost, was a first attempt to free myself from the chains of the "merely personal," from an existence which is dominated by wishes, hopes, and primitive feelings. Out yonder there was this huge world, which exists independently of us human beings and which stands before us like a great, eternal riddle, at least partially accessible to our inspection and thinking. The contemplation of this world beckoned like a liberation, and I soon noticed that many a man whom I had learned to esteem and to admire had found inner freedom and security in devoted occupation with it. The mental grasp of this extrapersonal *(ausserpersonlichen)* world within the frame of the given possibilities swam as the highest aim half consciously and half unconsciously before my mind's eye.

("Autobiographical Notes" 3–5)

It is striking to note how words like "eternity" and "liberation" enter Einstein's remarks as a matter of course. What he says about some of the characteristics of a serious scientist can be said as truly about a serious aspirant on a spiritual path. The attempt to free oneself from the chains of the merely personal in order to be available to the world of objective perception and thought is central for both. For Einstein, then, an engagement with science was a matter of spiritual vocation, a response to an inner call, a way of freeing oneself from one's egocentricity.

Einstein viewed science on a very large scale. For him it had to concern itself not only with the nature of the physical world, but also with the fate of humanity, with existence, and with reality. It was not just a workaday occupation but a way to pursue transcendent aspirations, a way through which he sought to understand "the secrets of the Old One." In an "Address at Columbia University," he remarked:

> It is, of course, universally agreed that science has to establish connections between the facts of experience, of such a kind that we can predict further occurrences from those already experienced. Indeed, according to the opinion of many positivists the completest possible accomplishment of this task is the only end of science.
>
> I do not believe, however, that so elementary an ideal could do much to kindle the investigator's passion from which really great achievements have arisen. Behind the tireless efforts of an investigator there lurks a stronger, more mysterious drive: it is existence and reality that one wishes to comprehend.
>
> (*Essays in Science* 112–3)

Of Planck he said, "The state of mind that enables a man to do work of this kind is akin to that of the religious worshipper or the lover; the daily work comes from no deliberate intention or programme, but straight from the heart" (*Essays in Science* 5). On another occasion he said, "Certain it is that a conviction, akin to religious feeling, of the rationality or the intelligibility of the world lies behind all scientific work of a higher order" (*Essays in Science* 11). It is clear that Einstein is not using the phrase "religious feeling" in any churchly sense; he means a feeling of awe, mystery, subtlety, and vastness—a feeling which in another context he called a "cosmic religious feeling."

If it is true that a great scientist and a great spiritual aspirant both seek objective perceptions in their attempts to comprehend existence and reality and that both of them are guided by something akin to religious faith in the possibility of such comprehension, then what is it that distinguishes them and marks them on apparently divergent paths? It is my impression that the fundamental distinction lies in the direction to which they look in pursuing their aims; the attendant means of investigation naturally vary.

Traditional spiritual aspirants, such as those who follow the path of Yoga or of Zen, or of the Prayer of the Heart, seek truth within, whereas scientists seek it outside. The methods and procedures for understanding nature inside a human being are, of course, different from those appropriate for studying nature outside. "Nature" here refers to all there is, known or unknown, without a distinction between what is "natural" and what is "supernatural"—a sense in which Spinoza, Goethe, and Einstein understood the word.

We cannot here discuss the different procedures relevant to these two directions for approaching nature. It seems worthwhile, however, to remark that in both cases a subtle interplay between theory and observation is involved. Both approaches are intellectual as well as empirical; in one case the confirmation of an idea is sought in external experiment, while in the other this confirmation is sought in internal experience. In both cases we get metaphors of truth: either as scientific theories and explanations or as religious symbols and scriptures.

In the external approach of science, only those aspects of reality are likely to receive attention that lend themselves to precise quantitative measurement. The general area of emotions, and more importantly the higher and more inclusive feelings like love, compassion, or a sense of purpose, may become objects of scientific scrutiny, but must be strictly excluded as instruments of that scrutiny. There may be aspects of reality that are perceptible only to the intelligence of the faculty of feelings, which measures quality and value rather than quantity, but science by definition excludes this faculty as an instrument of its method. Without this self-limitation, science could never have arrived at its own particular achievements.

The tragedy is that popular awe of science has led to the devaluation of the function of feeling as a means of arriving at any aspect of the truth, and as a consequence the quality of feeling in the culture has declined to the level of the infantile or brutal. The mistaken conviction that those limited aspects of reality that are accessible to science constitute the whole has become so deeply ingrained in us that it maintains its tenacious hold even against reason itself, which proposes to us that the most complete view of reality possible for human beings must be that which includes the perceptions of all the faculties, and all the faculties perfected to the highest possible degree.

With scientific instruments, such as the telescope or the microscope, we see more facts, or new facts, but we see them with our ordinary eyes. Our seeing is extended but not transformed; our organs of perception are enlarged but not cleansed.

In science, a change of vision comes about through a new, often more general or simpler, theoretical formulation which provides a different point of view so that the same facts are now seen in a different light, or new facts are seen which could not have been suspected before and were therefore not attended to. Scientific theories are ways of channeling attention; a new theory is like a new shaft of light bearing the possibility of revealing hidden facts. This new view is arrived at indirectly, through the agency of reasoning.

"Seeing" in science is basically interpretation. This becomes more and more apparent in contemporary physics, where most of the experimental work is performed using instruments that no longer simultaneously involve the object "seen" and our eyes. We infer many things indirectly about the object, and have confidence in our inferences owing to a logical consistency in our theories and a postulated consistency in nature, but we by no means always perceive the object directly. Thus not only theory but even experiments and "observations" are mediated by reason.

Reality as revealed by science is not directly experienced by feeling or sensation; it is indirectly conjectured by thought. However, scientific speculation undergoes a remarkable and continual self-correction through the subjection of its inferences to repeated experimental checks.

Self-correction also exists in the realm of the internal approach to reality. Here the intersubjective verification is more subtle and more qualitative, being based, not on quantitative measurement or statistics, but on the recognition of a description of inner experience by another who has passed through the same experience and of the external signs of an inner change of being. The unanimity with which the stages of development of an aspirant are assessed in genuine spiritual disciplines of all times and places suggests that this intersubjective verification is no less precise than that which exists in the realm of science, though it is of a different nature.

In the inner approach, theory is verified by direct self-observation and inner experience. A change of vision comes about through the transformation of the investigator himself or herself, and hence of the organs of perception. The person is both the instrument and the object of scrutiny. In perfecting this instrument, an individual, at the same time, extends and deepens the field of observation.

What is needed for objective perception is freedom from oneself. The spiritual aspirant escapes the personal self, not by ignoring it, but by attending to it with total honesty, thus establishing a consciousness which is independent of it and which, unlike the turbid medium of personal consciousness, is capable of becoming directly aware of the presence of the nonpersonal—or rather both suprapersonal and intrapersonal—Self of the self. The instrument, the whole person, undergoes a process of transformation brought about by the suffering entailed in the facing of one's inner contradictions and the subsequent voluntary subordination of the personal self to the greater Self discovered within.

The perceptions involved in internal knowing are direct and immediate. Understanding here includes poetic and intuitive insight as well as empirical and rational considerations. Far from being opposed to scientific and rational knowledge, it opens up even vaster and richer dimensions of reality, adding significance to science itself.

It seems strange, in the light of what has been said above, that people of good sense should regard the internal and external paths as opposing each other, rather than as mutually supportive and complementary. After all, the domain of nature, by which I simply mean all there is, includes what is inside human beings as well as what is outside. The spiritual aspirant's concern to know the self—both the ordinary self and the nonpersonal Self of all that exists—and the scientist's concern to know the world may be estranged halves of a primordial, unified search for knowledge expressed in the ancient idea that a human being as a micro-cosm mirrors in principle the macrocosm. How can an individual know himself or herself without recognizing this relatedness with the rest of the cosmos? And what point would there be if a person knew all about the stars and yet knew nothing essential about the self directly?

I think that the major cause of the imagined opposition between the two paths lies in the different faculties involved in the change of percep-tion. In both cases there is a firm conviction that reality is not as it appears to our ordinary senses. In the external approach of science, the change of vision is brought about primarily through the agency of reason, whereas in the internal approach, it is brought about mainly through feeling. Goethe was right in calling mysticism a dialectic of feeling; science, on the other hand, is a dialectic of reason. As Einstein remarked, "In a man of my type the turning-point of the development lies in the fact that gradually the major interest disengages itself to a far-reaching degree from the mo-mentary and the merely personal and turns towards the striving for a mental grasp of things" ("Autobiographical Notes" 7).

Wisdom must consist in a reconciliation of the various parts of one's own soul. An integration of the intellectual and the mystical or of science and religion as Einstein understood them (without meaning thereby anything denominational or institutional) is essential for the healing of our whole culture. It is important to stress, however, that the primary reconciliation that is needed is not of science and religion as abstractions. What is needed is a harmonization of the scientific and religious aspirations in the same person. The locus of reconciliation is within the soul of a single human being. The more an individual is inte-grated in the various faculties, the wiser such a person is likely to be, in whatever specialty one is engaged, whatever the particular calling is and whatever the capacities are.

What makes any career a spiritual path are the breadth of view with which one understands its purpose and the motives for which one pur-sues it. So long as an occupation is primarily motivated by ambition for self-advancement and self-aggrandizement, or by fear and insecurity, or by gratification of personal pleasure and inclinations, it cannot become a spiritual path. Freedom from oneself is a necessary prerequisite for apprehending reality as it is, rather than as we wish it to be.

Freedom from one's personal subjectivity, however, is not obtained by appealing to a collective subjectivity that remains an extension of oneself in a horizontal plane. Real objectivity seems to include an altogether different dimension. When Christ says, "He who would follow me must leave self behind," he is calling for movement along a vertical axis of being. In this connection it is worth recalling a remark of Einstein's as well: "The true value of a human being is determined primarily by the measure and the sense in which he has attained liberation from the self" (*Ideas and Opinions* 12).

As far as Einstein is concerned, we can say with confidence that for him science was a spiritual path, whereas on any path—scientific, religious, or artistic—the vast majority are no doubt self-seekers, more or less. Perhaps it cannot be otherwise. But, one cannot have a wood consisting of nothing but creepers:

> . . . science can only be created by those who are thoroughly imbued with the aspiration toward truth and understanding. This source of feeling, however, springs from the sphere of religion. To this there also belongs the faith in the possibility that the regulations valid for the world of existence are rational, that is, comprehensible to reason. I cannot conceive of a genuine scientist without that profound faith. The situation may be expressed by an image: Science without religion is lame, religion without science is blind. (*Ideas and Opinions* 46)

A SCIENCE OF INNER TRANSFORMATION

Is there a need for transformation? Is there anything wrong with us as we are? Is transformation a good thing? Is it like hot tubs, something that is selling these days in California, that we might as well sign up for? All the "with it" people are into transformation, as the young say. Transformation is the contemporary talisman—or should one say *mantra*—for success. Therefore, it is worth asking: "Why do we need transformation?"

A young man spoke to me recently after a talk I had given on the differences between the nature of perception in physics and that in Yoga. He told me with great excitement that quantum mechanics has proved the truths of the spiritual traditions, and he showed me a Lagrangian (a kind of mathematical function) published in an advertisement in the *New York Times*, which he insisted represented the Ultimate transformed state because this Lagrangian was bigger than anybody else's. One would gather from him and many other young people I meet these days that Bell's Theorem and the Tao are conspiring together to make physicists the high priests of transformation. Should the physics textbooks now be viewed as manuals of spiritual transformation and the physics professors as the roshis and gurus who themselves are transformed and can pronounce on these matters *ex laboratora*?

All this would auger well for physics. But, ironically, the number of applicants for graduate studies in physics keeps declining. Perhaps this is understandable: Since presumably the physicists have already achieved what the Buddha taught, we need something else more interesting. Of course, with the addition of a little "complexity" or "chaos," we might get a renewal of license in these matters for a little while longer! It is sad that so many young people place their hopes of personal and social transformation in the latest interpretation of one scientific theory or the other and refuse to look at themselves directly to discover what needs to be transformed and why.

When there is a discussion of transformation, usually it concerns the transformation of consciousness. However, there is a tendency to ignore the intimate link between "consciousness" and "conscience" (Ravindra, "Can Consciousness Survive"). Higher consciousness cannot exist without higher conscience. In many languages, such as French, Spanish, and Sanskrit, there is only one word for both "consciousness" and "conscience." This should itself suffice to indicate the very close connection between the two.

In the faith-centered biblical traditions, the emphasis is on the various levels of conscience, whereas in the insight-centered traditions of the Orient, the emphasis is on the various levels of consciousness. The former is more closely associated with feeling and the latter with the intellect. Consequently, it is easier for scientists or scientifically oriented intellectuals to focus on levels and transformation of consciousness rather than of conscience.

However, it is part and parcel of every spiritual tradition that there has to be a cultivation of the integration and harmonization of the body (will), head (intellect), and the heart (feelings). There is a celebration of both love and knowledge in all the traditions. And it is interesting to note that in the majority of the reports of near-death experiences, the beings of light commend and express both love and knowledge.

In old-fashioned terms, at least in the Christian context, it was said (for example quite strongly by Kierkegaard) that the best human beings can do is to recognize their sinfulness and their nothingness. Everything else follows from this recognition in the arena of transformation. If I see that I am sinful, I wish to repent, and so I work for salvation. If I see that I am nothing, I wish to be, and so I undertake the discipline of transformation.

To generalize a little, every spiritual tradition has said, in one way or another, that human beings do not live the way they should and could. The Christian way of putting it is that human beings live in sin but they can be saved and live in grace. The Hindu-Buddhist way of saying much the same thing is that we live in a state of sleep or of illusion but we can wake up and live in reality rather than in fantasy.

Some General Obstacles

Spiritual traditions have proposed ways, methods, disciplines, yogas, *tariqua*, or paths by which human beings can learn to live rightly. But religions by and large are not interested in these transformational disciplines, which, in general, require far too much effort to have mass appeal.

Because the hard paths have so little mass appeal, religions have often made concerns about spiritual transformation or higher levels of consciousness (and conscience) into matters of faith or prizes in a heavenly lottery. Sometimes, they have done so from a particular theological or metaphysical perspective on the relationship between human effort and Divine grace. We see striking examples of this in many Protestant Christian sects. Since they believe that no human action can possibly coerce the grace of God to descend, nothing one can do—however good or bad—is considered relevant to salvation. Therefore, said Martin Luther, "Sin bravely!" Or, following Calvin, we should behave in a manner indicating that we are among the elect who have already been saved. But, no matter what we do, we cannot be saved by our efforts.

A similar conclusion can also be reached from quite a surprisingly different source, such as in the teaching of Jiddu Krishnamurti. What we know and what we need are so radically different from each other, in such completely different dimensions of being, that there is no way to get There from here. Therefore, according to him, no process—no teaching or teachers, no tradition or method or yoga—is necessary or will result in transformation. This denial of process acts as an obstacle in the development of a science of transformation.

Both the Buddha and the Christ did have disciples; they taught so that others might be transformed. Something can be communicated, some instruction can be given, aspirants can be helped and ways of transformation can be practiced. At least some of the wisdom gathered by humanity in matters of our inner life can be conveyed by appropriate teachings.

It is true that the Uncaused Freedom (Nirvana) cannot be brought about by human ingenuity or actions (karma), but one can attempt to remove the impediments that hinder the descent of grace from Above. Patañjali's *Yoga Sūtras* (4.2–3) puts it so aptly, with a quiet balance: "Any transformation into a state of being is the result of fullness of Nature unfolding inherent potential. The apparent causes of a transformation do not in fact bring it about. They merely remove the obstacles to natural growth, as a farmer clears the ground for his crops."

Another obstacle to a transformation of conscience and consciousness is sectarian exclusivism. And this can have a very subtle origin: a deep-seated feeling that my way alone is true. A consciousness convinced that there can be only one expression of the Great Truth, or that there can only be one way to the summit of the Mountain, is bound to sabotage in clever ways any attempt to see the salient common features of a science of inner transformation.

It is important to appreciate that no spiritual path can be true if it is essentially devised, like the tower of Babel, here below by human reasoning. A true path depends on the Will of Heaven; it originates from Above. There cannot be a way from here to There, unless it is laid down from There to here. In these matters, more than elsewhere, it is true, as the Gospel says, "No one can lay hold on anything unless it is given him from on high" (John 3.27).

In spite of the various obstacles to the development of a science of inner transformation, such a science exists, and it is very ancient. It is necessary that in the emerging planetary culture such science be nonsectarian.

THE NEED FOR TRANSFORMATION

The need for transformation arises when one sees, as is attested in all spiritual disciplines in their own specific language and metaphors, that each one of us lives at the level of more or less complete imprisonment in self-occupation. These disciplines also all speak of a level of total freedom and attention to which human beings can aspire, and for whose sake they have been willing to undergo great hardships. The best human beings have always striven for a connection with the truth that transcends their egotistic requirements. They see the need for transformation because they see their fragmentation and the lack of internal unity, coherence, and order.

We don't do what we wish to do. St. Paul expresses the general human condition in Romans 7.15, 19: "I cannot even understand my own actions. I do not do what I want to do but what I hate. . . . What happens is that I do, not the good I will to do, but the evil I do not intend." Similarly, Arjuna asks in the Bhagavad Gita (3.36), on behalf of all searchers, "Krishna, what makes a person commit evil, against his own will, as if compelled by force?" Across cultures and across centuries, serious people have seen the lack of inner unity in their lives; they have suffered the state of fragmentation.

The state of fragmentation, of spiritual blindness, is quite natural; and, as Krishna says, it is the inherent tendency of nature which makes us turn like a machine. The real obstacle to transformation arises if we claim to see when we don't in fact see. Every great teacher has said words to the effect that we have eyes but we do not see, that we have ears but we do not hear. Coherence and order and internal unity do not belong to ordinary human beings; these are characteristics of a transformed person. Mere wishing to be compassionate like the Buddha will not do. I can read Dante and hope to be at a place where "my will and my desire were one with Love, the Love that moves the sun and the other stars" (*Divine Comedy*, canto 33.145). Wishing and hoping are always countered by denying and fearing. What is needed is freedom from that entire level of being. For that a payment is needed—the sacrifice of clinging to what I am.

SCIENCE OF INNER TRANSFORMATION

The fundamental requirement for any such science is impartial self-observation or self-objectivity. This is not easy, for owing to fear and self-importance, one is constantly fantasizing about one's true nature. Although fear and self-importance manifest themselves according to each person's particularity, gradually one recognizes that these are characteristics of a level of consciousness and need not be taken personally.

If we persist in self-inquiry, we discover more and more that deeper down we each express the human condition. In our depth, we see that the first person singular is in fact the First Person Universal. This progressively *objective* view is more and more *inner* but less and less *subjective.* It is important to emphasize this, for we have acquired a custom—mostly contributed by the natural sciences—that *objective* must be *external* and that what is *inner* is *subjective.* In our usage here, *objective* and *subjective* refer to different levels of perception, not to the location of what is perceived.

Because we take everything personally, we are quick to blame or to take credit and to make excuses for ourselves. Self-justification and rationalization make each one of us believe that I am the center of the universe and that the galaxies so turn that I am always right. The fantasy world of my own making can always be rearranged to bring me on top and to prove me right. We may or may not be *rational* beings by nature, as Aristotle claimed, we are certainly *rationalizing* beings!

Only when we are done with excuses—and the accompanying blaming of society, our times, our culture, or our parents, in short "them"—can we seriously look at ourselves impartially. Our nature reflects a level of consciousness and is nothing personal. Although each one of us expresses this level in our own particular manifestation, we are driven by forces and laws operating at the level where we are. We are suspended in a large-scale play of forces, but we can take it all too personally. As Shakespeare said, a young man's fancy turns to thoughts of love in the spring. But each young man regards himself to be uniquely situated with respect to the springtime fluttering of his heart.

The dragon that St. George struggles with has his own face. But even this is nothing personal. What stands in the way of inner order is an attachment to disorder. This attachment to disorder is an attachment to what is known, however bad. From our fear of loss of security and from our self-occupation with pleasures, ambition, and greed, we cling to what we know. The Buddha also struggled with these in his encounters with Mara, the Tempter, as did the Christ in his temptations in the wilderness. At our level, it is not quite so grand. The devils with whom we have to struggle correspond to our own level of being; they are rather small like us. Bigger devils are needed to struggle with bigger souls (Ravindra, *Christ the Yogi*, 81–3).

Much of the time we are self-occupied. The major manifestation of this self-occupation is fantasy, fear, anxiety, and worry. We worry. In fact,

Descartes's dictum "I think, therefore I am" has much less universality than "I worry, therefore I am"!

Fear, self-occupation, and worry are all indications of the tyranny of time over our consciousness. They show how we live in the past or the future, fleeing from the present.

There is a deep-seated inner contradiction at our very core. We most fear what we most desire. We wish for transformation, but we fear it. We wish to be transformed without changing, without losing anything. Thus transformation becomes a matter of another achievement—to be added to our accomplishments—while deep down we remain the same self-centered person, convinced that my purposes and enhancement are separate from the projects and enhancement of the rest of the cosmos.

Clinging to this isolated self (in Sanskrit, *asmitā*, "I am this" or "I am that")—rather than participating in the fullness of being as I AM—is the first product of ignorance according to the *Yoga Sūtras*. It is the root of self-importance and of fear. It is the very thing from which we need to be freed. We more and more see that freedom is not *for* myself, but *from* myself. As is said in ancient Indian texts, anyone who is someone cannot come to the "Sun door."

All traditions speak about a major difficulty of transformation. Recall again the struggles of the Buddha and of Jesus Christ. They speak about the necessity of dying to one's fears and ambitions, dying to what one is, dying to the world, and dying to oneself, in order to be born of the spirit into a new mode of being.

To be born anew, we need to participate in the great flow of energies that exist all around us, rather than merely to be an isolated and therefore stagnant reservoir. For this purpose, the various spiritual disciplines emphasize right posture (not only physically but emotionally), right breathing (recall the relationship of "breath" with spirit in so many ancient languages), and good works.

The self-observation mentioned above is naturally transformative and yields deepening self-knowledge. There is a very intimate relationship between knowing and being. The English word *realize* connotes both of these aspects, and one can say that self-knowledge gradually leads to Self-realization. Realization of the Self—which in some contexts is what is understood as soul or as spirit—comes into existence only as a result of impartial self-knowledge and from the transformation of energy usually locked up in one's ordinary self.

This point of view avoids the fruitless opposition of the fundamental tendencies of existentialism and the natural sciences, on the one hand, and of essentialist perspectives of religion and metaphysics, on the other. One may or may not have an eternal "soul" to start with, but one can, through a systematic and rigorous pursuit of a science of inner transformation, realize a Self that participates in the level of eternity. This is how one is born of the Spirit, or in the Spirit, or with the Spirit.

This is also the way one gives birth to the Spirit, to the Word, or to Christ. Many saints and mystics have spoken about the requirement to be impregnated by the Spirit in order to give birth to Christ. So Angelus Silesius said, "Christ could be born a thousand times in Galilee. But all in vain if he is not born in me."

One cannot say, "I did it." It is all done, not by, but through me. One does what must be done, not for one's own glory, nor according to one's self-will, but for the Will of Him Who sent me. Like Arjuna, one engages in the struggle for *dharma* for the maintenance of the world order, in accordance with the purposes of Krishna. So too, the Buddha said, "Look within; you are the Buddha!" And like the Christ, one could say, "The Father and I are one" (John 10.30).

SCIENCE AND THE MYSTERY OF SILENCE

When I consider thy heavens, the work of thy fingers,
the moon and the stars, which thou hast ordained,
what is man, that thou art mindful of him?

(Psalm 8)

Throughout human history, in every age and culture, whenever human beings have been struck by the grandeur of the cosmos and its workings, they have wondered what place they have in it. What meaning can our life, with all its limitations and smallness, have in the midst of very large forces operating in the universe? Is our Earth significant when galaxies are continuously emerging and dissolving? Are the "three score and ten years" of our existence, or the "hundred years," as the Vedas say, meaningful in the context of the billions of years of cosmic expansion and contraction? What purpose does our life have when each year, one hundred million of us, on average, die? We die and are replaced by others, like you and me, with our ambitions, fears, and hopes. Why? For what?

Every human being sometimes wonders about the universe in which we live, about its vastness, about the variety of manifestations in it, about the endless transformations of substances and energies, and the intricate laws by which all this is regulated. That the universe exists is a wonder! And that it works and continues to exist is even a greater wonder.

Each one of us is thus some sort of a scientist. We may not undertake investigations of the cosmos and the forces and laws governing it rigorously or in any systematic manner. But we can hardly be uninterested in the place where we have our being, where the Spirit manifests itself, where all the aesthetic possibilities are realized, and where precise intellectual formulations find their concrete expression.

Moreover, not to wonder about one's own existence—its meaning, function, and purpose—is that possible? Unless one is determinedly partial and fragmented, one could hardly be oblivious either to the mystery of one's own existence, or to the mystery of the cosmos. Both mysteries exist, perhaps parts of one larger mystery. In the vastness of the universe, I am a small particle, a mere nothing! But, equally true, I am the center of my cosmos. What is myself?

How am I related with all there is? What perception is needed for me to hold the truths of my nothingness and of my centrality in a proper perspective? These and such questions are not new; they are as old as humankind. In different forms and languages—myths, ideas, colors, musical notes, sculpture—these questions have engaged human beings everywhere.

When we are driven by the necessities of survival, or by assertions of our ambitious egos, we may forget these questions for short or long periods. But something in us is always deeply unsatisfied unless we keep returning to some form of inquiry about our own nature and our relationship with others and the cosmos. Who am I? Why am I here?

It is hard to imagine an intelligent human being who is not interested simultaneously in the entire psychosomatic complex of the cosmos and the animating spirit behind it. Whether one considers this at the scale of an individual body-mind-soul or at the scale of the whole universe and the Cosmic Spirit, neither the perceived nor the perceiver can be ignored.

In the language of the Bhagavad Gita (13.2), "knowledge of the field and of the knower of the field is true knowledge." In Sanskrit, other words that are often used to describe the two realms are *prakriti* and *purusha*. *Prakriti* is nature in all its various aspects and levels of subtlety, including also the subtle psychic and parapsychic phenomena; it is the total domain of materiality and laws, everything that can become an object of study or thought or perception.

Purusha, on the other hand, is the perceiver, the self, and the spirit. Just as there is an underlying unity behind all natural entities and processes, all having arisen from common subtle matter obeying the same laws, there is an underlying unity behind all the knowing selves or consciousnesses. Individual consciousnesses are differentiated from a larger common consciousness through different mind-bodies, the material instruments of perception and action.

One of the resounding affirmations of the Upanishads is that *ātman* is *Brahman*. This is one of what are called "the great utterances" *(mahāvākya)* in the Indian tradition: In essence, the individual consciousness is identical with the consciousness of the All. Or, as Krishna (the highest Purusha) says to Arjuna (who symbolizes an awakening individual consciousness), "know me as the Knower of the Field in all fields" (Bhagavad Gita 13.2).

Anyone who wishes to know Krishna must learn to know his own innermost self, for Krishna is not any particular being, born at this or that place, of this or that form or shape or color, but the innermost and the highest Purusha who is seated in the heart of everyone, the essential Self of all selves. He is represented in dark colors precisely because he is mysterious and unknown. He is often painted blue because he is vast as the sky or the ocean, as is our own Self, which is declared by the Upanishads to be the same as Brahman (literally, the "Vastness").

The fact that Krishna is the essential Self of all selves needs to be emphasized, for otherwise he can become a sectarian god in competition with others, as Jesus Christ has become in Christianity. The biblical Christ is a true messenger of the highest God, who like the Upanishadic sages says that he is one with the Father *(ātman* is *Brahman)*, and in order to follow whom, we have to leave our ordinary selves aside and delve deeper into our forgotten Ground. But Christians generally put an ordinary self on him with particularities of name, form, and place, and turn him into a sectarian miracle worker in whom they then believe with all the exclusivism and emotional vehemence of a frightened man, substituting believing for seeing and the crutch of dogma for the sword of gnosis.

However paradoxical it may appear on the surface, to come to one's own innermost self (Krishna or Christ), most of us need guidance and instruction. The various spiritual paths and disciplines, often quite varied in their emphases and methods owing to the different periods and places of their development and different types of psyches to which they are addressed, aim at precisely this: to prepare seekers to come to and to stay in front of the naked truth in the deepest levels of their being, without fear and anxiety, which lead one to take up the crutches of some doctrine or belief.

The Zen master, D. T. Suzuki said, "Meditation opens the mind of man to the greatest mystery that takes place daily and hourly; it widens the heart so that it may feel the eternity of time and the infinity of space in every throb; it gives us a life within the world as if we were moving about in paradise; and all these spiritual deeds take place without any refuge into a doctrine, but by the simple and direct holding fast to the truth which dwells in our innermost being."

As long as a person is interested in both the spirit and its dwelling place, *Brahman* and *Brahmānda*, one's inner self and the cosmos, *purusha* and *prakriti*, the knower of the field and the field, the realm of purpose and that of action, one cannot but be interested in both spiritual traditions and science. Although, as the Bhagavad Gita (13.26) says, all existences, moving or unmoving, arise from the union of the field and the knower of the field, human beings are particularly endowed with the possibility of the self-awareness of their real nature.

Self-awareness has many levels and is something that needs to be cultivated and deepened and should not be confused with any supposed characteristic of *Homo sapiens* which at some stage in history became a part of human nature and which is now automatically given at birth. Also, one must not fall into the easy temptation of thinking that since there is some sort of unity of spirit and body in all creatures, nothing needs to be understood further. To refer to the Bhagavad Gita (13.34) again, real discernment of the differences between the field and the knower of the field is essential for coming to the supreme goal of liberation.

It is also good to remind ourselves that any real reconciliation of the demands of the spirit and those of the body is not a matter of general mental abstractions such as "science" and "religion." It is only in a unique, particular, and individual soul that any such reconciliation has any meaning. It is only in the concrete existential situation in which we simultaneously experience and intentionally embrace the different forces of the two realms of spirit and body or religion and science that we have a possibility of wholeness. Otherwise, we remain fragmented, thinking about or wishing for wholeness.

However, there are occasions when we reflect, from the outside as it were, about science and religion as cultural and social endeavors, and consider their procedures and presuppositions, their similarities and differences. The first thing a person notices both about the spiritual traditions and about science is their internal diversity. Not all spiritual traditions are alike, any more than all sciences at different periods or in different cultures are exactly alike. Orthodox Brahmins for centuries struggled against the Buddha and the Buddhists.

In every tradition there have been many heretics; and many of them were far more passionate and divinely inspired about Truth or God than the orthodox. There is an inevitable hardening of any tradition with the passage of time, although clearly a tradition can be periodically renewed from within by those who are willing to seek beyond the dogmas and comforts of religions and who are able to recapture the original vibration of the impulse, often in a new form for a new age.

Ultimately a true child of God brings no new teaching. A true teaching is original but not novel, for wisdom that is eternal is not of time. It is the ancient way that is uncovered and revealed afresh for a new generation. "I have seen," the Buddha says, "the ancient way, the old road that was taken by the formerly All-Awakened, and that is the path I follow" (Samyutta Nikaya 2.106). Yajñavalkya, in the oldest Upanishad, quotes verses which were already old by his time, and which mention "the narrow path which stretches far away," by which "the wise are set free and ascend" (Brihadranyaka Upanishad 44.8). And nobody arrogates the honor of being a high priest to himself; he is called by God, as was Christ in the succession of Melchizedek (Hebrews 5.1–10).

Nevertheless, all teachings and great revelations degenerate; they get defiled by people like us—self-seeking and self-important. We move from inquiry to dogma, from exploration to explanation, and from spiritual paths to religions. In the process, we are once again trapped in beliefs and doubts, fears and desires. From seeking ways for freedom and love, we are captured by the means for possession and control. As in the ancient simile of the finger pointing to the moon, rather than achieving a transformation of our being so that we may come to the oneness of the moon of the spirit, we are continually occupied with the exclusivist finger of religions and sects.

Science too is not the same everywhere and at all times. The Chinese sciences and the European sciences are different from each other in their fundamental attitudes toward nature. Within Europe, there are profound differences in the procedures and assumptions of post-sixteenth-century modern science and earlier sciences. I have elsewhere tried to point out some of the presuppositions of modern science, which are persistent and continuous with contemporary sciences in spite of some major revolutions within modern science in the twentieth century (cf. chapter 7, "Experience and Experiment" in this volume).

Here, let me mention only three of these assumptions. The first one is that in modern science, in complete contrast to all traditional sciences, creation is assumed to be from below upward. Matter somehow came into existence, then, chronologically later and ontologically dependent on matter, arose intelligence, and later still, if it is admitted at all, somehow came the spirit. In that sense alone (and not in the sense of being interested only in the lower things of life) all scientists are professionally materialists; that is to say, they regard matter as prior to everything else and as the basis for everything that exists.

For scientists, it is the body that has the spirit, whereas in the traditional cosmologies, it is the spirit, which for its own purpose and according to natural (not supernatural but "subtle natural") laws, takes on a body. For example, in all the Indian languages, one would traditionally say that a person who has died "has given up the body." Presumably this person is now in another form of existence and may, if necessary according to the laws of *prakriti*, be reincarnated in another body. In a summary form, one might say that for the traditional cosmologies, matter is coarsened spirit, whereas for modern scientific cosmology, spirit is organized matter.

A second assumption of modern scientific procedures is that whatever is investigated is in principle capable of being subjected to control and manipulation by scientists and technologists. The subject matter under investigation may be an elementary particle, or another culture, or the human mind, or extrasensory perception, but the general scientific attitude is of manipulation and control. What does this insistence on control and manipulation amount to in knowing something? Does it not guarantee that we cannot know, by these methods, anything subtler or more intelligent than ourselves, anything that is higher than we are, if such a being or force is not susceptible to our control? If scientists speak of lacking evidence of anything higher than human beings, that is to be expected, for their procedures specifically preclude the possibility of any such evidence.

The third assumption is the fact that, according to the metaphysics of modern science, the state of being of scientists is irrelevant to the type of science they produce (Ravindra, "Modern Science"). A related assumption is that, given enough research grants, a scientist can so set the experiments that the actual collection of data, precisely where observation takes place, can be done by a computer. This is as true in experimental psychology as in physics. The state or the nature of the scientist is irrelevant to the observations, or more precisely, only those observations will be admitted into science to which the state of the scientist is irrelevant.

Whether it is the Buddha or an automaton collecting scientific data, only the aspects of their perceptions that are common to both will be accepted. In this impoverishment of our perceptions, the reverse principle naturally operates. Nothing in science can in principle change anybody's level of being; at least nothing in science as we know and practice it now. Change of a person's level of being, on the other hand, is the sole raison d'être of spiritual paths.

To point to these differences in some of the fundamental concerns and assumptions of contemporary sciences and the concerns of the spiritual traditions is not to say that an individual scientist cannot approach science in the spirit and attitude of a spiritual discipline. Science, like all other activities, has the possibility of being a spiritual way, a ladder connecting different levels of being, for its practitioners. A noteworthy contemporary example is that of Einstein. For him, certainly, an engagement with science was a matter of a spiritual vocation, a response to an inner call, a way of freeing himself from his egocentricity. But this attitude is as possible today as it was a hundred years ago, or three hundred years ago; and it is as little practiced now as it was then.

An integration of our intellectual and spiritual tendencies, or of science and religion as Einstein understood them—not denominational or institutional—is essential for healing ourselves and our whole culture. The primary reconciliation that is needed is, however, a harmonization of the various aspirations in the same person. The locus of reconciliation is within the soul of a single human being. The more an individual is integrated in the various faculties, the wiser that person is likely to be in all activities.

What makes any career a spiritual path is the breadth of view with which one understands its purpose and the motives for which one pursues it. So long as an occupation is primarily motivated by ambition for self-advancement and self-aggrandizement, or by fear and insecurity, or is undertaken for a gratification of personal pleasure and inclinations, it cannot become a spiritual path. Freedom from oneself is a necessary prerequisite for apprehending reality as it is, rather than as we wish it to be.

Freedom from one's personal subjectivity, however, is not obtained by appealing to a collective subjectivity. A collective subjectivity remains an extension of oneself in a horizontal plane. Real objectivity must include an altogether different dimension. When Christ says, "He who would follow me must leave self behind," he is calling for movement along a vertical axis of being. In this connection it is worth recalling a remark of Einstein as well: "The value of a human being is determined primarily by the measure and the sense in which he has attained liberation from the self" (*Ideas and Opinions* 12).

When science does serve as a spiritual path, then there are moments when one is bathed in the wonder of it all. One stays in front of the mystery in amazement. It is a mystery that broadens and deepens with contemplation. It is not a whodunit type of mystery, which will sooner or later be resolved by a new theory or a fresh clue or an innovative experiment. It cannot be resolved, but it can be loved and deepened. One comes to the mystery of oneself and the mystery of it all. One knows that one must ask questions, perhaps one must do science, just as some others must write poetry or make music. All this is being human, and precisely why the Old One, as Einstein occasionally called God, must be mindful of human beings. It is a part of our being human that some of us must theorize to go beyond theory, some must intellectualize to come to a stillness of the mind, and some of us must make music to come to the silence.

CHAPTER THIRTEEN

HEALING THE SOUL:
TRUTH, LOVE, AND GOD

Om! Lead me from untruth to Truth
Lead me from darkness to Light
And from death to Eternal Life.
(Brihadāranyaka Upanishad 1.3.28)

TRUTH AND REALITY

Who am I? Whence is this widespread cosmic flux?
These, the wise should inquire into diligently,
Soon—nay, now

(Mahopanishad 4.21)

When I consider thy heavens, the work of thy fingers,
The moon and the stars which thou hast ordained,
what is man, that Thou art mindful of him?

(Psalm 8)

Questions about human beings and their purpose are intimately connected with questions about the nature and meaning of the universe. Inquiry and search for Truth arise in the wonder and the beauty of existence. The sheer fact of being, the fact that the universe is and that there are human beings who can reflect upon this existence is a great mystery. Religion, science, and art all arise in our attempts to understand this mystery. Albert Einstein, the greatest scientist of the past century if not of all time, said, "Certain it is that a conviction, akin to religious feeling, of the rationality or the intelligibility of the world lies behind all scientific work of a higher order."

The Truth about ourselves and about the cosmos expresses itself in moral obligations and commandments (*Dharma* in India, *Tao* in China, and *Torah* in Palestine), social laws, and laws of nature. Lawfulness and order are the very essence of the cosmos—even etymologically as the Greek word *kosmos* means "order" and "ornament" as well as "universe." One of the insights of the great traditions has been that our inner nature is also lawful, even though the laws governing the inner nature are subtler than the ones we discover when we study external nature.

It is a well-nigh universal idea that a person who is fully developed is a microcosm that essentially mirrors the great cosmos. An implication of this idea is that the cosmos, in addition to its physical and biological aspects, also has spiritual aspects, as do human beings. In order to rigorously study these spiritual aspects—which are concerned with the meaning and significance of our existence, its purpose, and relationship with all there is—we must utilize means and procedures that are suitable to these aspects. These are the very procedures that are the concern of all spiritual disciplines.

One word means both "truth" and "reality" in Sanskrit, as in many other ancient languages. In the invocation at the beginning of this article, the word for "Truth," *sat*, is also "reality." Only the real is true, and truth alone is real. When we live in fantasy, imagining this or that, driven by fear or self-importance, truth is lost, and so are we. Thus we fall into darkness and fragmentation. Truth alone can bring us to light and make us whole. Nothing but the Whole can heal our soul; nothing short of the Vastness (Brahman) can make us whole, for as it has been said, "Our soul cannot find rest unless it is stayed in God."

The search for Truth may become more and more mental and divorced from deeper and higher feelings such as compassion, a sense of the oneness of the all, and the like. When that happens, the search leads to feelings of isolation and anxiety. Into this sense of isolation of oneself from all else—from other human beings as well as from the rest of nature—fear and self-importance enter. The silence of the vast spaces frightens us if we do not feel deeply that we belong to the entire cosmos. Much of our modern predicament arises from this very dedication to truth in an exclusively mental manner. Feelings of alienation of our selves as isolated egos naturally follow.

HEALING COMES FROM MOST HIGH

The soul is the very quality of aspiration that is oriented towards the Vastness and seeks to be related with It, much as a magnetic compass always seeks to orient itself toward the north pole. However, impediments, compulsions, and obstructing forces can interfere and one can be alienated from the Highest, which always and eternally resides in the deepest part of each being. Integration requires a spiritual discipline. Connecting with the Highest is the aim of all religions and spiritual paths, as is suggested by the etymologies of the words *religion* ("tying back") and *yoga* ("union"). All true healing comes from Most High, which is the same as to say from deep within.

The sages in all the great traditions have said in myriad ways that Love is a fundamental quality of the cosmos. Not only a quality but a basic constituent of Ultimate Reality. The Rig Veda (10.129.4) says, "In the beginning arose Love." And the New Testament affirms, "God is love, and he who abides in love abides in God, and God in him" (1 John 4.16). The search for this great Love at the very heart of the cosmos is both the beginning and the end of all spiritual paths, expressed as service, mercy, compassion, and ultimately oneness with all other beings. The core of all spiritual practice is freedom from the selfish, isolated, and isolating ego so that one can see more and more clearly and be related with all others more and more lovingly and selflessly. The great contemporary sage of India, Maharishi Ramana said simply, "There are no others." In the very last canto of the *Paradisio* in the *Divine Comedy*, Dante expresses his vision of the highest heaven:

> There my will and desire
> Were one with Love;
> The love that moves
> The sun and the other stars.

The great traditions, in wondrously different ways, have maintained that the Highest Reality—variously called "God," "First Principle," "Original Mind," or simply "That"—is Truth and Love. In our own days, Mahatma Gandhi maintained, almost like a practical spiritual equation, less to be preached and more to be lived, that God = Truth = Love. The

Theologia Germanica (ch. 31) says, "As God is simple goodness, inner knowledge, and light, he is at the same time also our will, love, righteousness and truth, the innermost of all virtues."

The realization of this truth, vouchsafed to the most insightful sages in all lands and cultures, is not something that can be abstracted, bracketed, or packaged. This insight needs to be continually regained, lived, and celebrated. Only when this realization is made concrete, is there an abundant life of the spirit. Spiritual disciplines are all concerned with integration and wholeness, above all with the integration of Truth and Love. Love is required to know Truth, and knowledge of Truth is expressed by Love. "The knower of truth loves me ardently," says Krishna in the Bhagavad Gita (7.17) and also "Only through constant love can I be known and seen as I really am, and entered into" (11.54). More contemporarily, the Archimandrite Vasileios of Mount Athos has said, "For if our truth is not revealed in love, then it is false. And if our love does not flow from the truth, then it is not lasting" (*Hymn of Entry* 26).

Of course, the search for Love can become merely a personal wish for my comfort and security, just as the search for Truth can become largely a technological manipulation of nature in the service of the military or of industry. Whenever truth and love are separated from each other, the result is either sentimentality or dry intellectualism, in which power is divorced from compassion. Partiality always carries seeds of violence and fear in it.

Thus in the name of "our loving God" many people have been killed, and many destructive weapons have been developed by a commitment to "pure knowledge." But such is not the best of humanity, either in the sciences or in religions. Integrated human beings in every culture and in every age have searched for both Truth and Love, insight and responsibility, wisdom and compassion. Above the mind, the soul seeks the whole, and is thus able to connect with wisdom and compassion.

Even in the great traditions, one can see different emphases. The insight- and truth-oriented traditions, such as Hinduism and Buddhism, have elaborate descriptions of various levels and states of consciousness, whereas in the faith- and love-oriented biblical traditions, the emphasis is much more on various levels of conscience. Examples of these differences can be found in two well-known traditional texts: *The Tibetan Book of the Dead* and Dante's *Divine Comedy*, both of which deal with the journey of the soul after death, and with the cultivation of the right quality of life.

If we examine this matter with critical sympathy, we will see that this major difference in the biblical and the Indic traditions—that of emphasis on conscience or on consciousness—is related to another major difference between the two main streams of spirituality. In the biblical traditions, the root cause of the human predicament is an assertion of the human self-will as opposed to the will of God, which has been revealed in his commandments. "Nothing burneth in hell except self-will," says the *Theologia Germanica* (ch. 34). And the whole exquisite agony of the cross—the way of the Christ—is in his last words in the Garden of Gethsemane: "If it is possible, let this cup pass me by. Yet, not my will, but thine be done" (Mark 14.36). In the Indic traditions, on the other hand, the root cause of the human difficulty is ignorance, which in its turn gives rise to suffering *(dukkha)* and to illusion *(māyā)*. In the biblical traditions, submission of our will in obedience to the will of God is called for; in the Indic tradition, the requirement is for the sword of gnosis *(jñāna)* which will cut the knot of ignorance.

Another fundamental difference follows from the former. In the Indic traditions, to hold on to a separate individuality in any ultimate sense is regarded as ignorance, whereas in the biblical traditions a lack of individuality—even in the presence of God—is seen as a lack of responsibility. In one case, the general traditional emphasis is very much on the oneness of all there is, whereas in the other case the emphasis is on the uniqueness of human beings from all other creatures and of each person with respect to one another.

The words "oneness" and "uniqueness" are derived from the same root; but their meanings diverge radically. The traditions that hold the ideal of oneness are insight-oriented and have developed a great deal of wisdom about various levels of consciousness. These levels always have to do with degrees of steadiness of attention and gradations of clarity of perception. The traditions extolling uniqueness are faith- and obedience-oriented and have a great deal to say about individual responsibility and moral conscience corresponding to the quality of virtuous conduct or the degrees and the gravity of sinfulness. Levels of consciousness are emphasized in one case, and levels of conscience in the other. (It hardly needs to be said that all the great traditions contain almost everything the other traditions have; the differences are largely in the mainstream emphases.)

It is possible, but neither generous nor insightful, to convince oneself that half the sages in the world have misunderstood the matter and only the other half have found the truth. Of course, once certain modes of expressions are used in a cultural and linguistic context, a traditional momentum develops. Only the modes and terms used by the great teachers in that tradition seem appropriate to their followers. This preference is not harmful by itself, but trouble arises when the dogmatic followers in any tradition insist that Truth can be expressed only in one form.

All the great teachers have said in one way or another that the experiences approaching God or Truth or Nirvana or Brahman or the Ultimate cannot be expressed in the language of the lower levels, and that a radical transformation of conscience-consciousness—a spiritual rebirth—is needed for us to experience the Real. The sages have articulated significant truths in different ways, often constrained by the abilities of their pupils and the specific language of discourse, emphasizing what they themselves found helpful.

The specificity of the language context cannot be overemphasized. In some cases, for example in French and Spanish, there is only one word corresponding to both the English words "consciousness" and "conscience" (French *conscience*, Spanish *conciencia*). The awakening of conscience is the feeling preparation for an enhancement of consciousness. It is not possible to come to a higher state of consciousness without coming to a higher state of conscience. On the other hand, those who are in touch with higher levels of consciousness naturally manifest largeness of heart. Inclusiveness and compassion identify a sage, just as a particular kind of fragrance indicates the presence of a rose.

The great traditions are always right, if they are understood rightly. But such traditions are almost always misunderstood, especially when taken externally and partially, with exaggerated emphasis on rational speculation or on sentimental devotion. If the traditions had not been misunderstood, Krishna, the Buddha, and the Christ would not have thrown such a forceful challenge at the official guardians of the traditions into which they were born. One sees not only that the traditions are continually betrayed, but also that the traditions themselves betray the Truth. Indeed, *tradition* and *treason* are from the same root, namely Latin *traditio:* "the act of handing over." Whenever a scholastic interpretation freezes a tradition into a rigid formulation, however liberating it had once been and however hallowed by time, one needs especially to recall the words of Krishna: "For a Brahmin [seeker of Brahman, the Vastness] who truly knows, there is as much use in all the Vedas [sacred texts] as there is in a well when there is a flood of water on all sides" (Bhagavad Gita 2.46).

HEALING THE SOUL

The soul is not only the arena of the struggle between our carnal nature and our spiritual nature, it is also the faculty of awareness of this struggle, manifesting primarily in the ability for self-reflection, and in an aspiration to be oriented to the whole. Although metaphysically speaking, one may wish to maintain that every human being by the very fact of being human has a potentiality for inner awareness or self-reflection, in practice, not many of us have the luxury or the requisite freedom from fear and self-importance to engage in much inner awareness. Thus, in a pragmatic sense, not all of us have a soul; and those who have it do not always have access to it.

On the other hand, our soul can be more and more refined; in other words, the ability of inner awareness can be cultivated. Much emphasis is placed in great traditions on attending to the inner world. The most ancient Upanishad, the Brihadranyaka (1.4.15) says, "Whoever departs from this world without having realized their own inner world, to them life has been of no service; it remains unlived, like the unrecited Vedas or any other undone deed."

A great deal of emphasis has been placed by the traditions on self-knowledge, the kind of knowledge that transforms and heals the soul. The words written over the ancient library of Ozymandias, the king of Egypt, meant "the Soul's Cure." Self-knowledge is a prerequisite to, if not synonymous with, knowledge of God. According to Plutarch (*Moralia*, 384 D.f.), the inscription at Delphi, "Know thyself," is an injunction addressed by God to all who approach Him. Human beings see "the nature of *Brahman* through the nature of their own self, as by a lamp," says the Shvetshvatara Upanishad (2.15). Plotinus (*Enneads* 5.3.9) said, "Those who seek to penetrate the nature of the Divine Mind must see deeply into the nature of their own souls, into the Divinest part of themselves." In fact, it appears that the only way to God is by self-knowing, dying to one's superficial self and being born to a deeper self. Clearly, there are differences in detail and emphasis, but there is no other point on which there is a greater unanimity of principle among the various masters of spiritual becoming. One of the noncanonical sayings of Jesus Christ is "The Kingdom of heaven is within you and whosoever knoweth the self shall find it. And having found it, ye shall know yourselves that ye are the sons and heirs of the Father, the Almighty, and shall know yourselves that ye are in God, and God in you. And ye are the City of God" (Happold, *Mysticism* 174–5).

Obviously, there are levels of self-knowledge that correspond to a development of or to a deepening of being. Different traditions refer to these levels in many ways: as a seven-storied mountain, as rungs of a ladder, or as levels of consciousness. Within ourselves at the level of ordinary humanity, where we usually are, there is confusion and chaos. We are like "a troubled sea, a sea that cannot rest, whose troubled waters cast up mud and filth" (Isaiah 57.20). We have conflicting desires, and our compulsions are in constant flux; there is nothing abiding, nothing that could be properly called "self." As Pascal said, "We are naught but lies, duplicity, contradiction, and we hide and disguise ourselves from ourselves" (*Pensées* 91).

Only deeper down is there the possibility of increased understanding, integration, and wholeness. Only in a state of collectedness, composure, openness, and alertness can we know anything objectively. In all other states our perceiving apparatus is out of tune and it introduces its own noise arising out of the internal or external distractions and afflictions. Nothing that we decipher in these dispersed states is ultimately trustworthy. One of the purposes of the various spiritual schools is to help human beings repair themselves so that they may gradually come to a state of preparedness, freed of subjective desires, expectations, and fears.

As long as we keep making our little noises, we cannot truly hear. Only when quieted within, may we encounter what is real.

In a purified and integrated state, arrived at after a long and arduous spiritual journey, we can discover our deepest self, which sages call by various names: "the spirit of the soul" (Eckhart), *acumen mentis* (Hugh of St. Victor), "center of the soul" (St. Teresa of Avila), "spark of the soul" (St. Jerome), "the divine person who is beyond the beyond" (Mundaka Upanishad). These are all attempts to name the nameless, but as Eckhart said, "The God who is without a name is inexpressible, and the soul in its ground is equally inexpressible, as He is inexpressible. . . . To gauge the soul we must gauge it with God, for the ground of God and the ground of the soul are one and the same" (Ancelet-Eustache, *Master Eckhart* 66).

Healing of the soul is both a finding of the soul and its refinement and right ordering, an attunement to that which is subtle and real and on which the manifest world is dependent. Transformative self-knowledge is thus both a discovering and a sculpting of the soul. Sages often declare such a soul to be eternal, always there from the beginning, but constantly threatened by fragmentation and perdition. To say that human beings are made in the image of God is a statement about the Real, not about the actual. For the actual to mirror the Real needs work and spiritual discipline, a Yoga. In the process of that work, the soul is healed as it finds its proper place in the Whole.

Healing of the soul quite naturally leads to the healing of our planet and, in fact, of the whole cosmos. The microcosmos-macrocosmos correspondence does not apply to every human being. It is only the fully developed person *(mahāpurusha)* who is said to mirror the whole cosmos. To become such a developed and whole person requires a transformation of the natural self. Then we discover not only that we are one with the cosmos in its physical and biological materiality and lawfulness, but also that the cosmos is one with us and has many inner and spiritual aspects.

In our attempts to find objective knowledge, which is the great aspiration of science, we cannot eliminate the person or the soul. What is needed, in fact, is an enlargement of the being of the person, freed from the merely personal and subjective. In order to truly comprehend, one needs to be comprehensive. This does not require a horizontal extension of more and more knowledge, but a vertical transformation that allows a participation in universal being. Such a transformed person is naturally inclusive and compassionate.

More and more, as the practice of a spiritual discipline frees us from fear and self-importance, we can come to clearer and clearer perceptions, so that we can see things as they really are, things of time as subsets of eternity. Such cleansed perceptions reveal objective reality, which surely includes, not only what we can measure, but also that which can take the measure of our own being. Such perceptions always carry a sense of universal significance derived from their participation in the Mystery. An example from William Blake's "Auguries of Innocence":

> To see a World in a Grain of Sand
> And a Heaven in a Wild Flower,
> Hold Infinity in the palm of your hand
> And Eternity in an hour.

Spiritual Yoga—whether of the East or of the West—is nonsectarian and inclusive. Thus Christ said, "Believe me, woman, an hour is coming when you will worship the Father neither on this mountain, nor in Jerusalem. . . . An hour is coming, and is already here, when those who are real worshippers will worship the Father in spirit and in truth. Indeed it is just such worshippers the Father seeks. God is spirit and those who worship Him must worship in spirit and in truth" (John 4.21, 23–4). Every spiritual Yoga aims at the realization of the transformed being, a *mahāpurusha*. Such persons are deeply in accord with their own inner core as well as with that of the cosmos, manifesting the First Person Universal. Such persons love what they know. Only such persons can know without opposition and separation, freed from any desire to control or to manipulate. A person whose soul is healed, that is to say, is whole, is naturally a sage.

Apart from the selflessness (and the accompanying absence of pride) and the natural feelings of compassion and love, which are characteristic of all the sages, there is one feature that is rarely remarked upon. A sage simultaneously sees the oneness of all things and the uniqueness of each thing. One cannot be unmindful of the seeming paradox here. However, we are speaking about the experience of the sages and not about the limitations of our ordinary minds.

It is a fact of their existence and behavior that, in relationship with others, the sages are aware that each human being is a manifestation of One Divine Energy, but that at the same time each person presents a unique potential (and corresponding particular difficulties) and is a wondrously unique expression of the Vastness. Each person is related with the oneness, but no person is replaceable by another. The One is unique in each manifestation. The sage sees everyone and everything as both one with the Source as well as uniquely themselves.

References

Ancelet-Eustache, Jeanne. *Master Eckhart and the Rhineland Mystics.* Trans. Hilda Graef. New York: Harper Torchbook, 1957.

Armstrong, A. Hilary, and Ravi Ravindra. "Dimensions of the Self: *Buddhi* in the *Bhagavad Gita* and *Psyché* in Plotinus." In *Yoga and the Teaching of Krishna: Essays on the Indian Spiritual Traditions*, ed. Priscilla Murray, 72–98. Adyar, Chennai (Madras), India: Theosophical Publishing House, 1998.

Augustine, Saint, Bishop of Hippo. *De Civitate Dei. The City of God against the Pagans.* Ed. and trans. R. W. Dyson. Cambridge: Cambridge University Press, 1998.

Burtt, Edwin Arthur. *The Metaphysical Foundations of Modern Science.* Garden City, N.Y.: Doubleday, 1954.

Einstein, Albert. "Autobiographical Notes." In *Albert Einstein: Philosopher-Scientist*, ed. P. A. Schilpp, 1:1–95. New York: Harper and Row, 1959.

———. *Essays in Science.* New York: Philosophical Library, 1934.

———. *Ideas and Opinions.* Based on *Mein Weltbild.* New York: Crown, 1954.

———. *Out of My Later Years.* New York: Philosophical Library, 1950.

Eliot, Thomas Sterns. "The Dry Salvages." In *Four Quartets*, 25–33. London: Faber and Faber, 1944.

Feynman, Richard Phillips. *The Feynman Lectures on Physics*, Vol. 1. Reading, Mass: Addison-Wesley, 1963.

Freud, Sigmund. *A General Introduction to Psychoanalysis.* Trans. Joan Riviere. Garden City, N.Y.: Garden City Pub., 1943.

Galileo Galilei. *Dialogue Concerning the Two Chief World Systems: Ptolemaic and Copernican.* 2d ed. Trans. Stillman Drake. Berkeley: University of California Press, 1967.

————. *Discoveries and Opinions of Galileo*. Trans. Stillman Drake. Garden City, NY: Doubleday, 1957.

————. *Le opere di Galileo Galilei*. Edizione Nazionale. 20 vols. Florence: G. Barbére. 1890–1909.

Happold, Frederick Crossfield. *Mysticism: A Study and an Anthology*. Harmondsworth: Penguin, 1967.

Holton, Gerald. *Thematic Origins of Scientific Thought*. Cambridge, Mass: Harvard University Press, 1973.

Krishnamurti, Jiddu. *Commentaries on Living*. First series. Ed. D. Rajagopal. Wheaton, Ill: Theosophical Publishing House, Quest Books, 1967.

Moore, Ruth. *Niels Bohr*. New York: Knopf, 1966.

Nasr, Seyyed Hossein. *The Encounter of Man and Nature: The Spiritual Crisis of Modern Man*. London: Allen and Unwin, 1968.

Pascal, Blaise. *Pensées*. Trans. H. F. Stewart. New York: Modern Library, 1967.

Patañjali. *Yoga: Discipline of Freedom: The Yoga Sutra Attributed to Patanjali*. Trans. Barbara Stoler Miller. Berkeley, Calif: University of California Press, 1996.

Planck, Max. *Where Is Science Going?* New York: Norton, 1932.

Pollard, E. C. "The Mystery of Life" [interview with E. C. Pollard]. *Yale Alumni Magazine* 18.6 (March 1955): 6–8.

Popper, Karl Raimund. *Conjectures and Refutations: The Growth of Scientific Knowledge*. New York: Basic Books, 1962.

Ravindra, Ravi. "Can Consciousness Survive Bodily Birth and Existence?" In *Yoga and the Teaching of Krishna: Essays on the Indian Spiritual Traditions*, ed. Priscilla Murray, 257–73. Adyar, Chennai (Madras), India: Theosophical Publishing House, 1998.

————. *Christ the Yogi*. Rochester, Vt.: Inner Traditions, 1998. Orig. pub. as *The Yoga of the Christ*, 1990.

———. "Einstein, Albert." In *The Encyclopedia of Religion*, ed. Mircea Eliade, 5:71–2. New York: Macmillan, 1987.

———. "Is Religion Psychotherapy?—An Indian View." In *Yoga and the Teaching of Krishna: Essays on the Indian Spiritual Traditions*, ed. Priscilla Murray, 99 –112. Adyar, Chennai (Madras), India: Theosophical Publishing House, 1998.

———. "Is the Eternal Everlasting?" In *Yoga and the Teaching of Krishna: Essays on the Indian Spiritual Traditions*, ed. Priscilla Murray, 238–48. Adyar, Chennai (Madras): Theosophical Publishing House, 1998.

———. "Kepler, Johannes." In *The Encyclopedia of Religion*, ed. Mircea Eliade, 8:275–6. New York: Macmillan, 1987.

———. *Krishnamurti: Two Birds on One Tree*. Wheaton, Ill.: Theosophical Publishing House, Quest Books, 1995.

———. "Modern Science and the Spiritual Paths." *American Theosophist* 68 (1980): 340–8.

———. "Newton." In *The Encyclopedia of Religion*, ed. Mircea Eliade, 10:414–5. New York: Macmillan, 1987.

———. "Physics and Religion." In *The Encyclopedia of Religion*, ed. Mircea Eliade, 11:319–23. New York: Macmillan, 1987.

———, ed. *Science and Spirit*. New York: Paragon House, 1991. Esp. ch. 1 "Introduction," by Ravi Ravindra; ch. 4 "The Hindu Attitude to Knowledge and Nature," by R. Balasubramanian; and ch. 5 "The Unity of Science and Spiritual Knowledge: The Islamic Experience," by Osman B. Bakar.

———. *Whispers from the Other Shore: Spiritual Search—East and West*. Halifax, Nova Scotia: Shaila Press, 2000.

———. "Yoga: the Royal Path to Freedom." In *Yoga and the Teaching of Krishna: Essays on the Indian Spiritual Traditions*, ed. Priscilla Murray, 52–71. Adyar, Chennai (Madras): Theosophical Publishing House, 1998.

Schroedinger, Erwin. *Nature and the Greeks*. Cambridge: Cambridge University Press, 1954.

————. *Science, Theory and Man*. New York: Dover, 1935.

Suzuki, Daisetz Treitaro. Quotation in *American Theosophist* 68 (1980): 312.

Vasileios, the Archimandrite. *Hymn of Entry*. Trans. Elizabeth Briere. Crestwood, N.Y.: St. Vladimir's Seminary Press, 1984.

Whitehead, Alfred North. *Science and the Modern World*. Lowell Lectures, 1925. New York: New American Library, 1958.

Wittgenstein, Ludwig. *Tractatus Logico-Philosophicus*. New York: Harcourt; London: Paul, Trench, Trubner, 1922.

INDEX

QUEST BOOKS
are published by
The Theosophical Society in America,
Wheaton, Illinois, 60189-0270,
a branch of a world fellowship,
a membership organization
dedicated to the promotion of the unity of
humanity and the encouragement of the study of
religion, philosophy, and science, to the end that
we may better understand ourselves and our place in
the universe. The Society stands for complete
freedom of individual search and belief.
For further information about its activities,
write, call 1-800-669-1571, e-mail olcott@theosmail.net
or consult its Web page: http://www.theosophical.org

The Theosophical Publishing House
is aided by the generous support of
THE KERN FOUNDATION,
a trust established by Herbert A. Kern
and dedicated to Theosophical education.

Praise for *Science and the Sacred*

I personally find this book captivating and mesmerizing. It is very important because it speaks not only to the spiritual and psychological health of humankind but to the survival of our planet. It is refreshing to read the opinions of a first-rate mind who is willing to unabashedly speak out about the primacy of spirit and to call into question many of the assumptions Western scientists make about the world, most of which go unchallenged in our culture.

> —Dr. Larry Dossey, MD, author of *Healing Beyond the Body* and *Recovering the Soul*

This is a significant contribution. . . . This book will certainly be of interest to the general public and all those concerned with the relationship between religion and science.

> —Dr. Seyyed Hossein Nasr, Professor of Islamic Studies, George Washington University: Gifford Lecturer, author of *Encounter of Man and Nature, Science and Civilization in Islam,* and *Sufi Essays*

Ravindra's exposition of the remarkable similarities and profound differences between the pursuit of science and the pursuit of spirituality goes to the heart of the matter. Complex issues are presented with delightful clarity. This seminal text is bound to exert a profound influence on any future treatment of the subject.

> —Dr. Shimon Malin, Professor of Physics, Colgate University, author of *Nature Loves to Hide: Quantum Physics and Reality, A Western Perspective*

A significant contribution to the fields of philosophy of science, comparative religion, and religious studies. A first-rate scholarly mind who also has considerable spiritual sensitivity deals with science without being intimidated by science.

> —Dr. Jacob Needleman, Professor of Philosophy, San Francisco State University, author of *The Heart of Philosophy, Lost Christianity, A Sense of the Cosmos,* and *Time and the Soul*